100

Best Delicious
Chocolate

The ultimate ingredient for tempting treats including 100 great recipes

First published in 2010
LOVE FOOD is an imprint of Parragon Books Ltd

Parragon
Queen Street House
4 Queen Street
Bath BA1 1HE, UK

ISBN: 978-1-4454-0383-0

Printed in China

Internal design by Fiona Roberts
Photography by Mike Cooper
Home Economy by Sumi Glass and Lincoln Jefferson
Introduction text by Linda Doeser

Notes for the Reader
This book uses both metric and imperial measurements. Follow the same units of measurement
throughout; do not mix metric and imperial. All spoon measurements are level: teaspoons are assumed
to be 5 ml, and tablespoons are assumed to be 15 ml. Unless otherwise stated, milk is assumed to be
full fat, eggs and individual vegetables are medium, and pepper is freshly ground black pepper.

The times given are an approximate guide only. Preparation times differ according to the techniques
used by different people and the cooking times may also vary from those given. Optional ingredients,
variations or serving suggestions have not been included in the calculations.

Recipes using raw or very lightly cooked eggs should be avoided by infants, the elderly, pregnant
women, convalescents and anyone suffering from an illness. Pregnant and breastfeeding women are
advised to avoid eating peanuts and peanut products. Sufferers from nut allergies should be aware
that some of the ready-made ingredients used in the recipes in this book may contain nuts. Always
check the packaging before use.

Contents

Introduction

'Blissful', 'heavenly', 'divine' or even 'to die for' – words of praise we immediately associate with this magical foodstuff. However, chocoholics of the twenty-first century are far from the first people to regard this unique, indulgent treat as precious and associate it with paradise. In the eighteenth century, the Swedish botanist Carolus Linnaeus, who devised a scientific system for classifying plants, named the cacao bush from which chocolate is produced *Theobroma* – food of the gods. Yet cocoa beans had been highly valued by the native people of Central and South America centuries before any European landed on its shores.

The Maya not only ate the sun-dried beans, probably ground to a paste and possibly mixed with water, but cultivated the bushes on which they grew. Depictions of the god *Ek-chuah* processing cocoa still exist today and it is also known that the Maya used the beans as a form of currency for trade before their civilisation died out in circa 900 AD. Further north in what is now Mexico, the Toltec people also valued the sun-dried beans and when they were conquered by the Aztec in 1325, cocoa beans became the currency of the new empire.

The World's Favourite Confectionery

The chocolate of today is very different from that of pre-Columbian America. The Aztecs had discovered that, if the beans fermented before they dried in the sun, they had a less bitter flavour. They also developed techniques for crushing, roasting, grinding and mixing the fat-rich cocoa paste with cold water. Chocolate was now a drink, served to kings and princes in gold cups.

In the sixteenth century, the Spanish conquistadors began to flavour the drink with spices from Spain and regarded it as a stimulant that improved the endurance of soldiers. It then became fashionable in Spain itself and its Caribbean colonies, but nowhere else, until the Italians became aware of it 100 years later and began to import cocoa beans. From there the fame of this now hot rather than cold drink, sometimes made with milk, spread throughout Europe. Fashionable chocolate houses appeared in all the major cities from Vienna to London and poems were written in praise of this elixir.

The transformation from drink to confectionery could not begin until the dawn of the Machine Age. Separating out the cocoa butter was the first stage in 1828, patented by Dutchman C. J. van Houten, and other developments followed, but it was Swiss confectioners who produced the first real 'eating' chocolate.

Types of Chocolate

The quality of chocolate depends on the quality of the raw ingredients and on the manufacturing process. As a general rule, the higher the percentage of cocoa butter, the better the flavour and texture of the product – and the higher the price. Good chocolate should be even in texture with no grains or specks and should have a distinctive chocolate taste rather than a flavour of cocoa. It should melt on the tongue and not feel sticky or greasy. With the exception of couverture (see below), all types of chocolate are made in varying quality.

✳ Milk chocolate has added milk solids, usually about 14 per cent, and milk fats. It is quite sweet with up to 55 per cent sugar and is light brown in colour.

✳ Plain chocolate is dark brown and only lightly sweetened.

✳ Dark chocolate is very dark, sometimes almost black, and is very lightly sweetened.

✳ Couverture is always high-quality plain or dark chocolate designed for cooking, icing and making confectionery. It has a high percentage of cocoa butter, which makes it very workable, but it must be tempered before use. This involves heating and cooling to specified temperatures and then working the chocolate with a metal spatula.

✳ White chocolate is not strictly chocolate because it is made from cocoa butter but contains no cocoa solids. It is more accurately known as white confectionery coating, but you are unlikely to see it advertised in this way on supermarket shelves.

✳ Chocolate-flavoured cake covering has a high proportion of vegetable fat and is low in cocoa butter. It melts easily and is low in price, but the flavour is poor and it is not recommended for the recipes in this book.

✳ Cocoa powder is usually unsweetened and is widely used in baking. Drinking chocolate is not a substitute because it has a much milder flavour and contains sugar.

Chocolate Heaven

Chocolate Fudge Cake

SERVES 8

To make the icing, put the chocolate, sugar, butter, evaporated milk and vanilla essence in a heavy-based saucepan. Heat gently, stirring constantly, until melted. Pour into a bowl and leave to cool. Cover with clingfilm and leave to chill for 1 hour, or until spreadable. Preheat the oven to 180°C/350°F/Gas Mark 4. Grease and line two 20-cm/8-inch cake tins.

To make the cake, put the butter and sugar in a bowl and beat until light and fluffy. Gradually beat in the eggs. Stir in the syrup and ground almonds. Sift the flour, salt and cocoa into a bowl, then fold into the mixture. Add a little water if necessary to make a dropping consistency. Spoon the mixture into the prepared tins and bake in the oven for 30–35 minutes, until springy to the touch and a skewer, inserted into the centre, comes out clean.

Remove the cakes from the oven, leave in their tins for 5 minutes, then turn out on to wire racks to cool. When the cakes are completely cold, sandwich them together with half of the icing. Spread the remaining icing over the top and sides of the cake, swirling it to give a frosted appearance.

175 g/6 oz butter, unsalted for preference, softened, plus extra for greasing
175 g/6 oz caster sugar
3 eggs, beaten
3 tbsp golden syrup
3 tbsp ground almonds
225 g/8 oz self-raising flour
pinch of salt
40 g/1$\frac{1}{2}$ oz cocoa powder

ICING
225 g/8 oz plain chocolate, broken into pieces
100 g/3$\frac{1}{2}$ oz dark muscovado sugar
225 g/8 oz butter, unsalted for preference, diced
5 tbsp evaporated milk
$\frac{1}{2}$ tsp vanilla essence

Chocolate Ganache Cake

SERVES 10

Preheat the oven to 180°C/350°F/Gas Mark 4. Lightly grease and line a 20-cm/8-inch springform cake tin. Beat the butter and sugar until light and fluffy. Gradually add the eggs, beating well after each addition. Sift the flour and cocoa together. Fold into the cake mixture. Fold in the melted chocolate.

Pour into the prepared tin and smooth the top. Bake in the preheated oven for 40 minutes, or until springy to the touch. Leave the cake to cool for 5 minutes in the tin, then turn out on to a wire rack and leave to cool completely. Cut the cake into 2 layers.

To make the ganache, place the cream in a saucepan and bring to the boil, stirring. Add the chocolate and stir until melted. Pour into a bowl, cool, then chill for 2 hours, or until set and firm. Whisk the mixture until light and fluffy.

Reserve one-third of the ganache. Use the remaining ganache to sandwich the cake together and spread over the top and sides of the cake.

Melt the cake covering and spread it over a large sheet of baking paper. Leave to cool until just set. Cut into strips a little wider than the height of the cake. Place the strips around the edge of the cake, overlapping them slightly.

Pipe the reserved ganache in tear drops or shells to cover the top of the cake. Leave to chill for 1 hour.

175 g/6 oz butter, plus extra
   for greasing
175 g/6 oz caster sugar
4 eggs, beaten lightly
250 g/9 oz self-raising flour
1 tbsp cocoa powder
50 g/1¾ oz plain chocolate,
   melted
200 g/7 oz chocolate-flavoured
   cake covering

GANACHE
450 ml/16 fl oz cream
375 g/13 oz plain chocolate,
   broken into pieces

Chocolate Truffle Torte

SERVES 10

Preheat the oven to 220°C/425°F/Gas Mark 7. Grease and line a 23-cm/9-inch springform cake tin. Put the sugar and eggs in a heatproof bowl set over a saucepan of gently simmering water. Whisk together until pale and resembling the texture of mousse. Sift in the flour and cocoa and fold gently into the mixture. Pour into the prepared tin and bake in the oven for 7–10 minutes, or until risen and firm to the touch.

Transfer to a wire rack to cool. Wash and dry the tin and replace the cooled cake in the tin. Mix together the coffee and brandy and brush over the cake. To make the truffle filling, put the cream in a bowl and whisk until just holding very soft peaks. Put the chocolate in a heatproof bowl set over a saucepan of gently simmering water until melted. Carefully fold the cooled melted chocolate into the cream. Pour the chocolate mixture over the sponge. Chill until set.

To decorate the torte, sift cocoa over the top and remove carefully from the tin. Using strips of card or greaseproof paper, sift bands of icing sugar over the torte to create a striped pattern. Cut into slices with a hot knife, to serve.

SPONGE

butter, for greasing
50 g/1¾ oz caster sugar
2 eggs
40 g/1¼ oz plain flour
25 g/1 oz cocoa powder
4 tbsp strong black coffee
2 tbsp brandy

TRUFFLE FILLING

600 ml/1 pint whipping cream
425 g/15 oz plain chocolate,
    broken into pieces

TO DECORATE

cocoa powder
icing sugar

Chocolate Cake with Syrup

SERVES 12

Preheat the oven to 190°C/375°F/Gas Mark 5. Grease and line a deep 20-cm/8-inch round cake tin. Place the chocolate, butter and coffee in a heatproof bowl and set over a saucepan of gently simmering water until melted. Stir to blend, then remove from the heat and leave to cool slightly.

Place the whole eggs, egg yolks and sugar in a separate bowl and whisk together until thick and pale. Sift the flour and cinnamon over the egg mixture. Add the almonds and the chocolate mixture and fold in carefully. Spoon the mixture into the prepared tin. Bake in the preheated oven for 35 minutes, or until the tip of a knife inserted into the centre comes out clean. Leave to cool slightly before turning out on to a serving plate.

Meanwhile, make the syrup. Place the coffee, sugar and cinnamon stick in a heavy-based saucepan and heat gently, stirring, until the sugar has dissolved. Increase the heat and boil for 5 minutes, or until reduced and thickened slightly. Keep warm. Pierce the surface of the cake with a cocktail stick, then drizzle over half the coffee syrup. Decorate with chocolate-covered coffee beans and serve, cut into wedges, with the remaining coffee syrup.

115 g/4 oz butter, plus extra
   for greasing
225 g/8 oz plain chocolate,
   broken into pieces
1 tbsp strong black coffee
4 large eggs
2 egg yolks
115 g/4 oz caster sugar
40 g/1½ oz plain flour
2 tsp ground cinnamon
85 g/3 oz ground almonds
chocolate-covered coffee beans,
   to decorate

SYRUP
300 ml/10 fl oz strong black
   coffee
115 g/4 oz caster sugar
1 cinnamon stick

Marble Cake

SERVES 10

Preheat the oven to 180°C/350°F/Gas Mark 4. Grease a 1.7-litre/3-pint ring mould. Put the chocolate and coffee in a heatproof bowl set over a saucepan of gently simmering water. Heat until melted. Leave to cool. Sift the flour and baking powder into a bowl. Add the butter, sugar, eggs, ground almonds and milk. Beat well until smooth.

Transfer one half of the mixture to another bowl and stir in the vanilla essence. Stir the cooled soft chocolate into the other half of the mixture. Place spoonfuls of the 2 mixtures alternately into the ring mould, then drag a skewer through to create a marbled effect. Smooth the top. Bake in the preheated oven for 50–60 minutes, until risen and a skewer, inserted into the centre, comes out clean. Leave in the mould for 5 minutes, then turn out on to a wire rack to cool.

To make the icing, put the chocolate, butter and water into a heatproof bowl set over a saucepan of simmering water. Heat until melted. Stir and pour over the cake, working quickly to coat the top and sides. Leave to set before serving.

225 g/8 oz butter, softened, plus
  extra for greasing
55 g/2 oz plain chocolate, broken
  into pieces
1 tbsp strong black coffee
280 g/10 oz self-raising flour
1 tsp baking powder
225 g/8 oz caster sugar
4 eggs, beaten
50 g/1¾ oz ground almonds
2 tbsp milk
1 tsp vanilla essence

ICING
125 g/4½ oz plain chocolate,
  broken into pieces
2 tbsp butter
2 tbsp water

Rippled Chocolate Gâteau

SERVES 10

Preheat the oven to 190°C/375°F/Gas Mark 5. Oil and line the bases of two 18-cm/7-inch shallow cake tins with greaseproof paper. Cream the butter, sugar and vanilla essence until light and fluffy. Add the eggs a little at a time, adding a little flour after each addition. When all the eggs have been added, stir in the remaining flour and the ground almonds. Add the cooled boiled water and mix lightly to form a smooth dropping consistency.

Melt the 25 g/1 oz of chocolate in a heatproof bowl set over a saucepan of gently simmering water. Stir until smooth, then pour over the cake mixture. Gently mix in a figure-of-eight action. Take care not to over-mix or the rippled effect will be lost. Divide between the 2 cake tins and smooth the tops. Tap lightly on the work surface to remove any air bubbles.

Bake in the preheated oven for 25–30 minutes, or until golden and the tops spring back when touched lightly with a finger. Remove from the oven and leave for 10 minutes before turning out on to a wire rack and discarding the lining paper. Leave until cold before icing.

To make the icing, place the chocolate in a heavy-based saucepan and add the butter and maple syrup. Heat gently, stirring frequently, until the chocolate has melted and the mixture is smooth. Add the sugar and stir gently until the mixture is well blended. Leave until cool and beginning to thicken. Beat occasionally during this time.

Split each cake in half and use one-third of the icing to sandwich the 4 layers together. Spread an additional third round the sides of the cake and roll in the flaked almonds. Spoon the remaining icing on top and spread with a swirling action to give a decorative effect. Sprinkle with the chocolate shavings to serve. Store in an airtight container.

1 tsp sunflower oil, for oiling
175 g/6 oz butter or margarine, softened
175 g/6 oz caster sugar
1 tsp vanilla essence
3 eggs, beaten
175 g/6 oz self raising flour
25 g/1 oz ground almonds
1–2 tbsp cooled boiled water
25 g/1 oz plain chocolate, broken into pieces

ICING
225 g/8 oz plain chocolate, broken into pieces
5 tbsp butter
2 tbsp maple or golden syrup
70 g/2½ oz dark muscovado sugar

TO DECORATE
40 g/1½ oz flaked almonds, toasted
chocolate shavings

Mocha Layer Cake

SERVES 8

Preheat the oven to 180°C/350°F/Gas Mark 4. Lightly grease three 18-cm/ 7-inch sandwich tins.

Sift the flour, baking powder and cocoa into a large mixing bowl. Stir in the sugar. Make a well in the centre and stir in the eggs, syrup, oil and milk. Beat with a wooden spoon, gradually mixing in the dry ingredients to make a smooth mixture. Divide the mixture between the prepared tins.

Bake in the preheated oven for 35–45 minutes, or until springy to the touch. Leave the cakes to cool in their tins for 5 minutes, then turn out on to a wire rack to cool completely.

To make the filling, dissolve the instant coffee in the boiling water and place in a bowl with the cream and icing sugar. Whip until the cream is just holding its shape. Use half of the cream to sandwich the 3 cakes together. Spread the remaining cream over the top and sides of the cake. Lightly press the chocolate shavings into the cream around the edge of the cake.

Transfer to a serving plate. Lay the caraque over the top of the cake. Cut a few thin strips of baking paper and place on top of the caraque. Dust lightly with icing sugar, then carefully remove the paper. Serve.

butter, for greasing
250 g/9 oz self-raising flour
1/4 tsp baking powder
4 tbsp cocoa powder
115 g/4 oz caster sugar
2 eggs
2 tbsp golden syrup
150 ml/5 fl oz sunflower oil
150 ml/5 fl oz milk

FILLING
1 tsp instant coffee powder
1 tbsp boiling water
300 ml/10 fl oz double cream
2 tbsp icing sugar

TO DECORATE
50 g/1¾ oz chocolate shavings
marbled chocolate caraque
icing sugar, for dusting

Chocolate Madeira Cake

SERVES 8–10

Preheat the oven to 180°C/350°F/Gas Mark 4. Lightly oil and line an 18-cm/7-inch cake tin with non-stick baking paper. Sift the flour and baking powder together and set aside.

Cream the butter with the sugar until light and fluffy, then gradually beat in the eggs, adding a little of the flour after each addition. When all the eggs have been added, stir in the remaining flour together with the ground almonds. Sift the drinking chocolate powder into the mixture and stir lightly.

Spoon the mixture into the prepared cake tin and smooth the top. Bake in the preheated oven for 50–55 minutes, or until a skewer, inserted into the centre, comes out clean. Remove from the oven and leave to cool before removing from the tin and discarding the lining paper. Leave until cold.

Sift the icing sugar and cocoa together into a mixing bowl and make a hollow in the centre. Place the butter in the centre. Mix with with sufficient hot water to form a smooth spreadable icing. Coat the top and sides of the cake with icing, swirling it to give a decorative effect. Dust with icing sugar.

1 tsp sunflower oil, for oiling
55 g/2 oz self-raising flour
1 tsp baking powder
115 g/4 oz butter or margarine, softened
115 g/4 oz caster sugar
3 eggs, beaten
25 g/1 oz ground almonds
115 g/4 oz drinking chocolate powder
1 tbsp icing sugar, for dusting

ICING
225 g/8 oz icing sugar
1½ tbsp cocoa powder
2 tbsp butter
3–4 tbsp hot water

Almond & Hazelnut Gâteau

SERVES 8

Preheat the oven to 190°C/375°F/Gas Mark 5. Grease two 18-cm/7-inch sandwich tins and line with greaseproof paper.

Whisk the eggs and caster sugar in a large mixing bowl with an electric whisk for about 10 minutes, or until the mixture is very light and foamy and a trail is left when the whisk is dragged across the surface.

Fold in the ground nuts. Sift the flour and fold in with a metal spoon or palette knife. Divide the mixture between the prepared tins.

Scatter the flaked almonds over the top of one of the cakes. Bake both of the cakes in the preheated oven for 15–20 minutes, or until springy to the touch.

Leave to cool slightly in the tins. Remove the cakes from the tins and transfer to a wire rack to cool completely.

Meanwhile, make the filling. Melt the chocolate, remove from the heat and stir in the butter. Leave the mixture to cool slightly. Whip the cream until just holding its shape, then fold in the melted chocolate until mixed.

Place the cake without the extra almonds on a serving plate and spread the filling over it. Leave the filling to set slightly, then place the almond-topped cake on top and chill for about 1 hour. Dust with icing sugar and serve.

butter, for greasing
4 eggs
115 g/4 oz caster sugar
50 g/1¾ oz ground almonds
50 g/1¾ oz ground hazelnuts
50 g/1¾ oz plain flour
70 g/2½ oz flaked almonds

FILLING
100 g/3½ oz plain chocolate, broken into pieces
1 tbsp butter
300 ml/10 fl oz double cream
icing sugar, for dusting

Mississippi Mud Pie

SERVES 8

To make the pastry, sift the flour and cocoa powder into a mixing bowl. Rub in the butter with the fingertips until the mixture resembles fine breadcrumbs. Stir in the sugar and enough cold water to mix to a soft dough in clingfilm. Wrap the dough and chill in the refrigerator for 15 minutes.

Preheat the oven to 190°C/375°F/Gas Mark 5. Roll out the pastry on a lightly floured work surface and use to line a 23-cm/9-inch loose-based flan tin or ceramic flan dish. Line with greaseproof paper and fill with baking beans. Bake in the preheated oven for 15 minutes. Remove the paper and beans from the pastry case and cook for a further 10 minutes until crisp.

To make the filling, beat the butter and sugar together in a bowl and gradually beat in the eggs with the cocoa powder. Melt the chocolate and beat it into the mixture with the single cream and the chocolate essence.

Reduce the oven temperature to 160°C/325°F/Gas Mark 3. Pour the mixture into the pastry case and bake for 45 minutes, or until the filling has set gently.

Let the mud pie cool completely, then transfer the pie to a serving plate. Cover with the whipped cream. Decorate the pie with chocolate flakes and curls and then chill until ready to serve.

PASTRY

225 g/8 oz plain flour, plus extra
   for dusting
2 tbsp cocoa powder
140 g/5 oz butter
2 tbsp caster sugar
1–2 tbsp cold water

FILLING

175 g/6 oz butter
350 g/12 oz soft dark brown
   sugar
4 eggs, lightly beaten
4 tbsp cocoa powder, sifted
150 g/5½ oz plain chocolate,
   broken into pieces
300 ml/10 fl oz single cream
1 tsp chocolate essence

TO DECORATE

425 ml/15 fl oz double cream,
   whipped
chocolate flakes and curls

Chocolate Crumble Pie

SERVES 8

To make the pastry, sift the flour and baking powder into a large bowl, rub in the butter and stir in the sugar, then add the egg yolk and the water to bring the dough together. Turn the dough out and knead briefly. Wrap the dough in clingfilm and chill in the refrigerator for 30 minutes.

Preheat the oven to 190°C/375°F/Gas Mark 5. Roll out the pastry and use to line a 23-cm/9-inch loose-based flan tin. Prick the base with a fork. Line with greaseproof paper, fill with baking beans and bake in the oven for 15 minutes. Remove the paper and beans. Reduce the oven temperature to 180°C/350°F/Gas Mark 4.

Bring the cream and milk to the boil in a saucepan, remove from the heat and add the chocolate. Stir until melted and smooth. Beat the eggs and add to the chocolate mixture, mix well and pour into the pastry case. Bake for 15 minutes, remove from the oven and leave to rest for 1 hour.

When you are ready to serve the pie, put the crumble topping ingredients into the food processor and pulse to chop. If you do not have a food processor, put the sugar in a large bowl, chop the nuts with a large knife and crush the biscuits, then add to the bowl with the cocoa and mix well. Sprinkle over the pie, then serve it in slices.

PASTRY

175 g/6 oz plain flour

1 tsp baking powder

115 g/4 oz unsalted butter, cut into small pieces

55 g/2 oz caster sugar

1 egg yolk

1–2 tsp cold water

FILLING

150 ml/5 fl oz double cream

150 ml/5 fl oz milk

225 g/8 oz plain chocolate, chopped

2 eggs

CRUMBLE TOPPING

115 g/4 oz soft light brown sugar

85 g/3 oz toasted pecan nuts

115 g/4 oz plain chocolate, chopped

85 g/3 oz amaretti biscuits

1 tsp cocoa powder

Chocolate Chiffon Pie

SERVES 8

Preheat the oven to 200°C/400°F/Gas Mark 6. Put the whole Brazil nuts in a food processor and process until finely ground. Add the granulated sugar and melted butter and process briefly to combine. Tip the mixture into a 23-cm/9-inch round flan tin and press it on to the base and side with a spoon or the fingertips. Bake in the preheated oven for 8–10 minutes until light golden brown. Set aside to cool.

Pour the milk into a heatproof bowl and sprinkle the gelatine over the surface. Let it soften for 2 minutes, then set over a saucepan of gently simmering water. Stir in half of the caster sugar, both the egg yolks and all the chocolate. Stir constantly over a low heat for 4–5 minutes, until the gelatine has dissolved and the chocolate has melted. Remove from the heat and beat until the mixture is smooth. Stir in the vanilla essence, pour into a bowl, cover with clingfilm and chill in the refrigerator for 45–60 minutes until starting to set.

Whip the cream until it is stiff, then fold all but about 3 tablespoons into the chocolate mixture. Whisk the egg whites in a separate, clean, grease-free bowl until soft peaks form. Add 2 teaspoons of the remaining sugar and whisk until stiff peaks form. Fold in the remaining sugar, then fold the egg whites into the chocolate mixture. Pour the filling into the pie case and chill in the refrigerator for 3 hours, or until set. Decorate the pie with the remaining whipped cream and the chopped nuts before serving.

NUT BASE
280 g/10 oz shelled Brazil nuts
4 tbsp granulated sugar
4 tsp melted butter

FILLING
225 ml/8 fl oz milk
2 tsp powdered gelatine
115 g/4 oz caster sugar
2 eggs, separated
225 g/8 oz plain chocolate,
  roughly chopped
1 tsp vanilla essence
150 ml/5 fl oz double cream
2 tbsp chopped Brazil nuts,
  to decorate

Blackberry Chocolate Flan

SERVES 6

To make the pastry, sift the flour, cocoa powder, icing sugar and salt into a mixing bowl and make a well in the centre. Put the butter and egg yolk in the well and gradually mix in the dry ingredients, using a pastry blender or 2 forks. Knead lightly and form into a ball. Wrap the dough and chill in the refrigerator for 1 hour.

Preheat the oven to 180°C/350°F/Gas Mark 4. Roll out the pastry on a lightly floured work surface. Use it to line a 30 x 10-cm/12 x 4-inch rectangular flan tin and prick the pastry case with a fork. Line the base with greaseproof paper and fill with baking beans. Bake in the preheated oven for 15 minutes. Take out of the oven and remove the paper and beans. Set aside to cool.

To make the filling, put the cream and jam in a saucepan and bring to the boil over a low heat. Remove the saucepan from the heat and stir in the chocolate and then the butter until melted and smooth. Pour the mixture into the pastry case and set aside to cool.

To make the sauce, put the blackberries, lemon juice and caster sugar in a food processor and process until smooth. Strain through a nylon sieve into a bowl and stir in the cassis. Set aside.

Remove the flan from the tin and place on a serving plate. Arrange the remaining blackberries on top and brush with a little of the blackberry and liqueur sauce. Serve the flan with the remaining sauce on the side.

PASTRY

140 g/5 oz plain flour, plus extra
  for dusting
25 g/1 oz cocoa powder
55 g/2 oz icing sugar
pinch of salt
85 g/3 oz butter, cut into small
  pieces
½ egg yolk

FILLING

300 ml/10 fl oz double cream
175 g/6 oz blackberry jam
225 g/8 oz plain chocolate,
  broken into pieces
25 g/1 oz unsalted butter, cut
  into small pieces

SAUCE

675 g/1 lb 8 oz blackberries, plus
  extra to decorate
1 tbsp lemon juice
2 tbsp caster sugar
2 tbsp crème de cassis

Toffee Chocolate Puff Tarts

MAKES 12

Line the bases of a 12-hole non-stick muffin tin with discs of greaseproof paper.

Cut out twelve 5 cm/2-inch circles from the edge of the pastry and cut the remainder into 12 strips. Roll the strips to half their thickness and line the sides of each hole with 1 strip. Put a disc of pastry in each base, and press well together to seal and make a tart case. Prick the bases and chill in the refrigerator for 30 minutes.

Preheat the oven to 200°C/400°F/Gas Mark 6. While the pastry is chilling, melt the chocolate in a heatproof bowl set over a saucepan of gently simmering water. Remove the bowl from the heat, cool slightly, then stir in the cream. Beat the sugar and egg yolks together and mix well with the melted chocolate.

Remove the muffin tin from the refrigerator and put a teaspoonful of the toffee sauce into each tart case. Divide the chocolate mixture between the tarts and bake in the preheated oven for 20–25 minutes, turning the tray around halfway through cooking, until just set. Remove from the oven and cool the tarts in the tin. Remove the tarts from the tin carefully, leaving behind the greaseproof paper. Dust with cocoa powder and serve with whipped cream.

375 g/13 oz ready-rolled puff pastry
140 g/5 oz plain chocolate, broken into pieces
300 ml/10 fl oz double cream
50 g/1¾ oz caster sugar
4 egg yolks
4 tbsp ready-made toffee sauce
cocoa powder, for dusting
whipped cream, to serve

Chocolate Mousse Tart

SERVES 8

To make the base, mix the digestive biscuits and amaretti biscuits with the butter and press well into the base of a 23-cm/9-inch springform cake tin. Chill in the refrigerator.

Melt the plain and milk chocolate in a heatproof bowl set over a saucepan of gently simmering water. Cool slightly, then add the egg yolks and mix well.

Whisk the egg whites until they form soft peaks, then add the caster sugar and whisk until stiff.

Fold the chocolate into the egg whites and pour over the biscuit base. Chill in the refrigerator for 8 hours, or overnight.

When you are ready to serve the tart, unmould it, transfer to a serving dish and crumble the chocolate flake bars over the top.

85 g/3 oz digestive biscuits, crushed
85 g/3 oz amaretti biscuits, crushed
70 g/2½ oz butter, melted

TOPPING
200 g/7 oz plain chocolate, broken into pieces
115 g/4 oz milk chocolate, broken into pieces
3 large eggs, separated
55 g/2 oz caster sugar
3 chocolate flake bars, to decorate

Black Forest Roulade

SERVES 8–10

Preheat the oven to 190°C/375°F/Gas Mark 5. Grease and line a Swiss roll tin with 1 whole sheet of greaseproof paper. Break the chocolate into small pieces and place in a heatproof bowl set over a saucepan of gently simmering water. Add the kirsch and heat gently, stirring until the mixture is smooth. Remove from the pan and set aside.

Place the eggs and sugar in a large heatproof bowl and set over the saucepan of gently simmering water. Alternatively, place in the heatproof bowl of a free-standing mixer and use a balloon whisk. Whisk the eggs and sugar until very thick and creamy and the whisk leaves a trail when dragged across the surface. Remove the bowl from the heat and whisk in the cooled chocolate.

Spoon into the prepared Swiss roll tin, then tap the tin lightly on the work surface to smooth the top. Bake in the preheated oven for 20 minutes, or until the top feels firm to the touch. Remove from the oven and immediately invert on to a whole sheet of greaseproof paper that has been sprinkled with the icing sugar. Lift off the tin and lining paper, then roll up, encasing the greaseproof paper in the roulade. Leave until cold.

For the filling, whip the cream until soft peaks form, then stir in the kirsch reserving 1–2 tablespoons. Unroll the roulade and spread over the cream to within 1/4 inch/5 mm of the edges. Scatter the cherries over the cream. Carefully roll up the roulade again and place on a serving platter.

1 tsp sunflower oil, for oiling
175 g/6 oz plain chocolate
2–3 tbsp kirsch or brandy
5 eggs
225 g/8 oz caster sugar
2 tbsp icing sugar, sifted

FILLING
350 ml/12 fl oz double cream
2-3 tbsp kirsch or brandy
350 g/12 oz fresh black cherries, stoned, or 400 g/14 oz canned morello cherries, drained and stoned

Crispy Chocolate Pie

SERVES 6

Preheat the oven to 160°C/325°F/Gas Mark 3. Grease a 20-cm/8-inch flan tin and base-line with greaseproof paper. Whisk the egg whites until stiff peaks form. Gently fold in the ground almonds, ground rice, caster sugar and almond essence. Spread the mixture over the base and sides of the prepared tin. Bake in the preheated oven for 15 minutes.

Meanwhile, put the chocolate in a heatproof bowl set over a saucepan of gently simmering water until melted. Remove from the heat and cool slightly, then beat in the egg yolks, icing sugar, whisky and the double cream until thoroughly incorporated.

Remove the flan tin from the oven and pour in the chocolate mixture. Cover with foil, return to the oven and bake at the same temperature for 20–25 minutes, until set. Remove from the oven and leave to cool completely.

Cut the pie into 6 slices. Decorate each slice with whipped cream and the marbled chocolate caraque. Serve immediately.

2 tsp butter, for greasing
2 egg whites
100 g/3$\frac{1}{2}$ oz ground almonds
4 tbsp ground rice
125 g/4$\frac{1}{2}$ oz caster sugar
$\frac{1}{4}$ tsp almond essence
225 g/8 oz plain chocolate,
   broken into small pieces
4 egg yolks
4 tbsp icing sugar
4 tbsp whisky
4 tbsp double cream

TO DECORATE
150 ml/5 fl oz whipped cream
marbled chocolate caraque

Chocolate Blueberry Tarts

MAKES 10

To make the pastry, put the flour, cocoa, sugar and salt in a food processor and pulse to mix. Add the butter, pulse again, then add the egg yolk and a little cold water to form a dough. If you do not have a processor, put the flour, cocoa, sugar and salt in a large bowl and rub in the butter until the mixture resembles breadcrumbs. Add the egg and a little cold water to form a dough. Cover the pastry with clingfilm and chill in the refrigerator for 30 minutes.

Preheat the oven to 180°C/350°F/Gas Mark 4. Remove the pastry from the refrigerator and roll out on to a lightly floured work surface. Use to line ten 10-cm/4-inch tart cases. Freeze for 30 minutes, then bake in the oven for 15–20 minutes. Leave to cool.

Put the blueberries, cassis and icing sugar in a saucepan and warm through so the berries become shiny, but do not burst. Leave to cool.

For the filling, melt the chocolate in a heatproof bowl set over a saucepan of gently simmering water, then cool slightly. Whip the cream until stiff and fold in the soured cream and chocolate.

Transfer the tart cases to a serving plate and divide the chocolate filling between them, smoothing the surface, then top with the blueberries.

175 g/6 oz plain flour, plus extra
    for dusting
40 g/1½ oz cocoa powder
55 g/2 oz caster sugar
pinch of salt
125 g/4½ oz butter
1 large egg yolk
200 g/7 oz blueberries
2 tbsp cassis
10 g/¼ oz icing sugar, sifted

FILLING
140 g/5 oz plain chocolate,
    broken into pieces
225 ml/8 fl oz double cream
150 ml/5 fl oz soured cream

Cappuccino Soufflé Puddings

MAKES 6

Preheat the oven to 190°C/375°F/Gas Mark 5. Grease the sides of six 175-ml/ 6-fl oz ramekin dishes with butter and coat with the extra caster sugar. Place on a baking tray. Place the cream in a saucepan and warm gently. Stir in the coffee until dissolved, then add the Kahlúa. Divide the mixture among the prepared ramekin dishes.

In a clean, greasefree bowl, whisk the egg whites until soft peaks form, then gradually whisk in the caster sugar until stiff and glossy but not dry. Put the chocolate in a heatproof bowl set over a saucepan of gently simmering water until melted. Add the egg yolks to the melted chocolate, then stir in a little of the whisked egg whites.

Gradually fold in the egg whites. Divide the mixture between the ramekins. Cook in the preheated oven for 15 minutes until just set. Dust with cocoa powder and serve immediately.

butter, for greasing
25 g/1 oz caster sugar, plus extra for coating
6 tbsp whipping cream
2 tsp instant espresso coffee granules
2 tbsp Kahlúa
3 large eggs, separated, plus 1 extra white
150 g/5½ oz plain chocolate, broken into pieces
cocoa powder, for dusting

Chocolate Queen of Puddings

SERVES 4

Preheat the oven to 180°C/350°F/Gas Mark 4. Break the chocolate into small pieces and place in a saucepan with the chocolate-flavoured milk. Heat gently, stirring until the chocolate melts. Bring almost to the boil, then remove the saucepan from the heat.

Place the breadcrumbs in a large mixing bowl with 25 g/1 oz of the sugar. Pour over the chocolate milk and mix well. Beat in the egg yolks.

Spoon into a 1.2-litre/2-pint ovenproof dish and bake in the preheated oven for 25–30 minutes or until set and firm to the touch.

Whisk the egg whites in a large greasefree bowl until soft peaks form. Gradually whisk in the remaining caster sugar and whisk until you have a glossy, thick meringue.

Spread the black cherry jam over the surface of the chocolate mixture and pile the meringue on top. Return the dish to the oven for about 15 minutes or until the meringue is crisp and golden.

50 g/1¾ oz plain chocolate
450 ml/16 fl oz chocolate-
   flavoured milk
100 g/3½ oz fresh white or
   wholemeal breadcrumbs
125 g/4½ oz caster sugar
2 eggs, separated
4 tbsp black cherry jam

Baked to Perfection

Double Chocolate Muffins

MAKES 12

Preheat the oven to 200°C/400°F/Gas Mark 6. Line a 12-cup muffin tin with muffin paper cases. Sift the flour, cocoa, baking powder and cinnamon into a large mixing bowl. Stir in the sugar and 125 g/4½ oz of the white chocolate.

Place the eggs and oil in a separate bowl and whisk until frothy, then gradually whisk in the milk. Stir into the dry ingredients until just blended. Spoon the mixture into the paper cases, filling each three-quarters full. Bake in the preheated oven for 20 minutes, or until well risen and springy to the touch. Leave to cool for 2 minutes, then remove the muffins and transfer to a wire rack to cool completely.

Melt the remaining white chocolate in a heatproof bowl set over a saucepan of gently simmering water until melted and spread over the top of the muffins. Leave to set, then dust the tops with a little cocoa and serve.

200 g/7 oz plain flour
25 g/1 oz cocoa powder, plus
   extra for dusting
1 tbsp baking powder
1 tsp ground cinnamon
115 g/4 oz caster sugar
185 g/6½ oz white chocolate,
   broken into pieces
2 eggs
100 ml/3½ fl oz sunflower oil
225 ml/8 fl oz milk

Chocolate Chip Muffins

MAKES 12

Preheat the oven to 200°C/400°F/Gas Mark 6. Line a 12-cup muffin tin with muffin paper cases.

Place the margarine and sugar in a mixing bowl and beat with a wooden spoon until light and fluffy. Beat in the eggs, yogurt and milk until combined.

Sift the flour and bicarbonate of soda into the mixture. Stir until just blended.

Stir in the chocolate chips, then spoon the mixture into the paper cases and bake in the preheated oven for 25 minutes, or until a fine skewer inserted into the centre comes out clean. Leave the muffins to cool in the tin for 5 minutes, then turn out on to a wire rack to cool completely.

3 tbsp soft margarine

200 g/7 oz caster sugar

2 large eggs

150 ml/5 fl oz natural yogurt

5 tbsp milk

280 g/10 oz plain flour

1 tsp bicarbonate of soda

175 g/6 oz plain chocolate chips

Chocolate Orange Muffins

MAKES 8–10

Preheat the oven to 190°C/375°F/Gas Mark 5. Line a 10-cup muffin tin with muffin paper cases.

Sift the flours in a mixing bowl and add the ground almonds and sugar.

Mix together the orange rind and juice, the cream cheese and the eggs. Make a well in the centre of the flour mixture and stir in the liquid, then add the chocolate chips. Beat well to combine all the ingredients.

Spoon the mixture into the paper cases, filling them no more than three-quarters full.

Bake in the centre of the preheated oven for 20–25 minutes, or until well risen and golden brown.

Leave to cool slightly on a wire rack, but eat them as fresh from the oven as possible.

oil, for greasing
125 g/4$\frac{1}{2}$ oz self-raising flour
125 g/4$\frac{1}{2}$ oz self-raising
   wholemeal flour
25 g/1 oz ground almonds
55 g/2 oz soft brown sugar
rind and juice of 1 orange
175 g/6 oz cream cheese
2 eggs
55 g/2 oz plain chocolate chips

Spiced Chocolate Muffins

MAKES 12

Line a 12-cup muffin tin with muffin paper cases.

Place the butter, caster sugar and brown sugar in a bowl and beat well. Beat in the eggs, soured cream and milk until thoroughly mixed. Sift the flour, bicarbonate of soda, cocoa and allspice into a separate bowl and stir into the mixture. Add the chocolate chips and mix well. Divide the mixture evenly between the paper cases. Bake in a preheated oven, 190°C/375°F/Gas Mark 5, for 25–30 minutes.

Remove from the oven and cool for 10 minutes, then transfer to a wire rack to cool completely. Store in an airtight container until required.

100 g/3½ oz butter, softened
150 g/5½ oz caster sugar
115 g/4 oz brown sugar
2 large eggs
150 ml/5 fl oz soured cream
5 tbsp milk
250 g/9 oz plain flour
1 tsp bicarbonate of soda
2 tbsp cocoa powder
1 tsp allspice
200 g/7 oz plain chocolate chips

Triple Chocolate Muffins

MAKES 12

Preheat the oven to 200°C/400°F/Gas Mark 6. Line a 12-cup muffin tin with muffin paper cases. Sift the flour, cocoa, baking powder and bicarbonate of soda into a large bowl, then stir in the plain and white chocolate chips.

Place the eggs, soured cream, sugar and butter in a separate mixing bowl and mix well. Add the wet ingredients to the dry ingredients and stir gently until just combined.

Using 2 spoons, divide the mixture between the paper cases and bake in the preheated oven for 20 minutes, or until well risen and firm to the touch. Serve warm or cold.

250 g/9 oz plain flour
25 g/1 oz cocoa powder
2 tsp baking powder
½ tsp bicarbonate of soda
100 g/3½ oz plain chocolate chips
100 g/3½ oz white chocolate chips
2 eggs, beaten
300 ml/10 fl oz soured cream
85 g/3 oz light muscovado sugar
85 g/3 oz butter, melted

Mocha Muffins

MAKES 12

Oil a 12-cup muffin pan with sunflower oil, or line it with 12 muffin paper cases. Sift the flour, baking powder, cocoa and salt into a large mixing bowl.

In a separate large bowl, cream the butter and Demerara sugar together, then stir in the beaten egg. Pour in the milk, almond essence and coffee, then add the coffee powder, chocolate chips and raisins and gently mix together.

Add the raisin mixture to the flour mixture and stir together until just combined. Do not overstir the mixture – it is fine for it to be a little lumpy.

Divide the muffin mixture evenly between the 12 cups in the muffin pan or the paper cases (they should be about two-thirds full). To make the topping, place the Demerara sugar in a bowl, add the cocoa and allspice and mix together well. Sprinkle the topping over the muffins, then transfer to a preheated oven, 190°C/375°F/Gas Mark 5, and bake for 20 minutes or until risen and golden. Remove the muffins from the oven and serve warm, or place them on a wire rack to cool.

1 tbsp sunflower oil or peanut
  oil, for oiling (if using)
225 g/8 oz plain flour
1 tbsp baking powder
2 tbsp cocoa powder
pinch of salt
115 g/4 oz butter, melted
150 g/5½ oz Demerara sugar
1 large egg, beaten
125 ml/4 fl oz milk
1 tsp almond essence
2 tbsp strong coffee
1 tbsp instant coffee powder
55 g/2 oz plain chocolate chips
25 g/1 oz raisins

COCOA TOPPING
3 tbsp Demerara sugar
1 tbsp cocoa powder
1 tsp allspice

Marshmallow Muffins

MAKES 12

Preheat the oven to 190°C/375°F/Gas Mark 5. Place 12 muffin paper cases in a muffin tin. Melt the butter.

Sift the flour, cocoa and baking powder together into a large bowl. Stir in the sugar.

Whisk the egg, milk and melted butter together, then gently stir into the flour mixture to form a stiff batter. Gently stir in the chocolate chips and marshmallows. Spoon the mixture into the muffin cases.

Bake the muffins in the preheated oven for 20–25 minutes, until well risen. Leave to cool in the tin for 5 minutes, then transfer to a wire rack and leave to cool completely.

70 g/2$\frac{1}{2}$ oz butter
280 g/10 oz plain flour
6 tbsp cocoa powder
3 tsp baking powder
85 g/3 oz caster sugar
1 egg, beaten
300 ml/10 fl oz milk
100 g/3$\frac{1}{2}$ oz milk chocolate chips
55 g/2 oz white mini marshmallows

Chocolate Brownies

MAKES 15

Preheat the oven to 180°C/350°F/Gas Mark 4. Grease and line a 28 x 18-cm/11 x 7-inch rectangular cake tin.

Put the butter and dark chocolate pieces into a heatproof bowl and set over a saucepan of simmering water until melted. Remove from the heat. Sift the flour into a large bowl, add the sugar and mix well. Stir the eggs into the chocolate mixture, then beat into the flour mixture. Add the nuts, sultanas and chocolate chips and mix well. Spoon evenly into the cake tin and level the surface.

Bake in the preheated oven for 30 minutes, or until firm. To check whether the cake is cooked through, insert a skewer into the centre – it should come out clean. If not, return the cake to the oven for a few more minutes. Remove from the oven and leave to cool for 15 minutes. Turn out on to a wire rack to cool completely. To decorate, drizzle the melted white chocolate in fine lines over the cake, then cut into squares. Leave to set before serving.

225 g/8 oz butter, diced, plus extra for greasing

150 g/5½ oz dark chocolate, chopped

225 g/8 oz self-raising flour

125 g/4½ oz dark muscovado sugar

4 eggs, beaten

60 g/2¼ oz blanched hazelnuts, chopped

60 g/2¼ oz sultanas

100 g/3½ oz dark chocolate chips

115 g/4 oz white chocolate, melted, to decorate

Double Chocolate Brownies with Fudge Sauce

MAKES 9 LARGE OR 16 SMALL

Preheat the oven to 180°C/350°F/Gas Mark 4. Grease and line an 18-cm/ 7-inch square cake tin. Place the butter and chocolate in a small heatproof bowl set over a saucepan of gently simmering water until melted. Stir until smooth. Leave to cool slightly. Stir in the sugar, salt and vanilla essence. Add the eggs, one at a time, until blended.

Sift the flour and cocoa powder into the mixture and beat until smooth. Stir in the chocolate chips, then pour the mixture into the prepared tin. Bake in the preheated oven for 35–40 minutes, or until the top is evenly coloured and a fine skewer inserted into the centre comes out almost clean. Leave to cool slightly while preparing the sauce.

To make the sauce, place the butter, sugar, milk, cream and syrup in a small saucepan and heat gently until the sugar has dissolved. Bring to the boil and stir for 10 minutes, or until the mixture is caramel-coloured. Remove from the heat and add the chocolate. Stir until smooth. Cut the brownies into squares and serve immediately with the sauce.

115 g/4 oz butter, plus extra
   for greasing
115 g/4 oz plain chocolate,
   broken into pieces
300 g/10½ oz caster sugar
pinch of salt
1 tsp vanilla essence
2 large eggs
140 g/5 oz plain flour
2 tbsp cocoa powder
100 g/3½ oz white chocolate chips

FUDGE SAUCE
4 tbsp butter
225 g/8 oz golden caster sugar
150 ml/5 fl oz milk
250 ml/9 fl oz double cream
225 g/8 oz golden syrup
200 g/7 oz plain chocolate,
   broken into pieces

Chocolate Fudge Brownies

MAKES 16

Preheat the oven to 180°C/350°F/Gas Mark 4. Lightly grease and line a 20-cm/8-inch square, shallow cake pan.

Beat together the cheese, vanilla essence and 5 teaspoons of caster sugar until smooth, then set aside.

Beat the eggs and remaining caster sugar together until light and fluffy. Place the butter and cocoa powder in a small pan and heat gently, stirring until the butter melts and the mixture combines, then stir it into the egg mixture. Fold in the flour and nuts.

Pour half of the cake batter into the prepared pan and smooth the top. Carefully spread the cheese mixture over it, then cover it with the remaining cake batter. Bake in the preheated oven for 40–45 minutes. Leave to cool in the pan.

To make the icing, melt the butter in the milk. Stir in the icing sugar and cocoa powder. Spread the icing over the brownies and decorate with pecan nuts, if using. Let the icing set, then cut into rectangles or squares to serve.

85 g/3 oz butter,
  plus extra for greasing
200 g/7 oz low-fat soft cheese
1/2 tsp vanilla essence
225 g/8 oz caster sugar
2 eggs
3 tbsp cocoa powder
100 g/31/2 oz self-raising flour,
  sifted
50 g/13/4 oz pecan nuts, chopped

FUDGE ICING
4 tbsp butter
1 tbsp milk
75 g/23/4 oz icing sugar
2 tbsp cocoa powder
pecan nuts, to decorate
  (optional)

Sticky Chocolate Brownies

MAKES 9

Preheat the oven to 180°C/350°F/Gas Mark 4. Lightly grease a 20-cm/8-inch square, shallow cake tin and line the base.

Place the butter, sugars, chocolate and golden syrup in a heavy-based saucepan and heat gently, stirring until the mixture is well blended and smooth. Remove from the heat and leave to cool.

Beat together the eggs and chocolate essence. Whisk in the cooled chocolate mixture. Sift together the flour, cocoa and baking powder and fold carefully into the egg and chocolate mixture using a metal spoon or palette knife.

Spoon the cake mixture into the prepared tin and bake in the preheated oven for 25 minutes, until the top is crisp and the edge of the cake is starting to shrink away from the tin. The inside of the cake will still be quite stodgy and soft to the touch.

Leave the cake to cool completely in the tin, dust with cocoa powder, then cut it into squares and serve.

85 g/3 oz butter, plus extra
  for greasing
140 g/5 oz caster sugar
100 g/3½ oz soft brown sugar
125 g/4½ oz plain chocolate,
  broken into pieces
1 tbsp golden syrup
2 eggs
1 tsp chocolate essence or vanilla
  essence
100 g/3½ oz plain flour
2 tbsp cocoa powder, plus
  extra for dusting
½ tsp baking powder

White Chocolate Brownies

MAKES 9

Preheat the oven to 180°C/350°F/Gas Mark 4. Lightly grease an 18-cm/7-inch square cake tin.

Roughly chop the chocolate and walnuts. Put 175 g/6 oz of the chocolate and the remaining butter in a heatproof bowl set over a saucepan of gently simmering water. When melted, stir together, then set aside to cool slightly.

Whisk the eggs and sugar together, then beat in the cooled chocolate mixture until well mixed. Fold in the flour, chopped chocolate and the walnuts. Turn the mixture into the prepared tin and smooth the surface.

Transfer the tin to the preheated oven and bake the brownies for about 30 minutes, until just set. The mixture should still be a little soft in the centre. Leave to cool in the tin, then cut into rectangles or sqaures before serving.

115 g/4 oz butter, plus extra
   for greasing
225 g/8 oz white chocolate
75 g/2¾ oz walnut pieces
2 eggs
115 g/4 oz soft brown sugar
115 g/4 oz self-raising flour

Marbled Chocolate Cheesecake Brownies

MAKES 12

Preheat the oven to 180°C/350°F/Gas Mark 4. Grease a 28 x 18-cm/11 x 7-inch rectangular baking tin.

Melt the butter in a medium saucepan, remove from the heat and stir in the cocoa and sugar. Beat in the eggs, then add the flour and stir to mix evenly. Pour into the prepared tin.

For the cheesecake mix, beat together the ricotta, sugar and egg, then drop teaspoonfuls of the mixture over the chocolate mixture. Use a palette knife to swirl the two mixtures together lightly.

Bake in the oven for 40–45 minutes, until just firm to the touch. Cool in the tin, then cut into rectangles or squares.

175 g/6 oz butter, plus extra
  for greasing
3 tbsp cocoa powder
200 g/7 oz caster sugar
2 eggs, beaten
125 g/4$\frac{1}{2}$ oz plain flour

CHEESECAKE MIX
250 g/9 oz ricotta cheese
40 g/1$\frac{1}{2}$ oz golden sugar
1 egg, beaten

Black Russian Brownies

MAKES 8–10

Preheat the oven to 180°C/350°F/Gas Mark 4. Grease and base-line a 30 x 20-cm/12 x 8-inch shallow cake tin with non-stick baking paper.

Melt the chocolate and the butter with the pepper in a small saucepan over a low heat. Remove from the heat and cool slightly.

Beat together the eggs, sugar and vanilla essence in a large bowl and stir in the chocolate mixture, Kahlùa and vodka.

Sift the flour and baking powder together and stir evenly into the chocolate mixture. Stir in the walnuts. Pour into the prepared tin and bake in the preheated oven for 20–25 minutes, until just firm to the touch.

Cool for a few minutes then cut into rectangles or squares and lift carefully from the tin on to serving plates.

For the topping, stir the Kahlùa into the crème fraîche and spoon a generous dollop on each brownie. Dust with a little cocoa powder and serve immediately.

115 g/4 oz butter, plus extra for greasing
115 g/4 oz plain chocolate, broken into pieces
$\frac{1}{2}$ tsp coarsely ground black peppercorns
4 eggs, beaten
250 g/9 oz caster sugar
1 tsp vanilla essence
3 tbsp Kahlùa liqueur
2 tbsp vodka
150 g/5$\frac{1}{2}$ oz plain flour
$\frac{1}{4}$ tsp baking powder
55 g/2 oz walnuts, chopped

KAHLUA TOPPING
2 tbsp Kahlùa
200 g/7 oz crème fraîche
cocoa powder, for dusting

Chocolate Butterfly Cakes

MAKES 12

Preheat the oven to 180°C/350°F/Gas Mark 4. Put 12 paper baking cases in a bun tray, or put 12 double-layer paper cases on a baking tray.

Put the margarine, sugar, flour, eggs and cocoa powder in a large bowl and, using an electric hand whisk, beat together until just smooth. Beat in the melted chocolate. Spoon the mixture into the paper cases, filling them three-quarters full.

Bake the cupcakes in the preheated oven for 15 minutes, or until springy to the touch. Transfer to a wire rack and leave to cool.

To make the filling, put the butter in a bowl and beat until fluffy. Sift in the icing sugar and beat together until smooth. Add the melted chocolate and beat together until well mixed.

When the cupcakes are cold, use a serrated knife to cut a circle from the top of each cake and then cut each circle in half. Spread or pipe a little of the butter cream into the centre of each cupcake and press 2 semi-circular halves into it at an angle to resemble butterfly wings. Dust with sifted icing sugar before serving.

125 g/4½ oz soft tub margarine
125 g/4½ oz caster sugar
150 g/5½ oz self-raising flour
2 large eggs
2 tbsp cocoa powder
25 g/1 oz plain chocolate, melted
icing sugar, sifted, for dusting

FILLING
85 g/3 oz butter, softened
175 g/6 oz icing sugar
25 g/1 oz plain chocolate, melted

Dark & White Fudge Cupcakes

MAKES 20

Preheat the oven to 180°C/350°F/Gas Mark 4. Put 20 paper baking cases in 2 bun trays, or put 20 double-layer paper cases on 2 baking trays.

Put the water, butter, sugar and syrup in a saucepan. Heat gently, stirring, until the sugar has dissolved, then bring to the boil. Reduce the heat and cook gently for 5 minutes. Remove from the heat and leave to cool.

Meanwhile, put the milk and vanilla essence in a bowl. Add the bicarbonate of soda and stir to dissolve. Sift the flour and cocoa powder into a separate bowl and add the syrup mixture. Stir in the milk and beat until smooth. Spoon the mixture into the paper cases until they are two-thirds full.

Bake the cupcakes in the preheated oven for 20 minutes, or until well risen and firm to the touch. Transfer to a wire rack and leave to cool.

To make the icing, break the plain chocolate into a small heatproof bowl, add half the water and half the butter, and set the bowl over a saucepan of gently simmering water until melted. Stir until smooth and leave to stand over the water. Repeat with the white chocolate and remaining water and butter. Sift half the icing sugar into each bowl and beat until smooth and thick. Top the cupcakes with the icing then leave to set. Serve decorated with chocolate shavings.

200 ml/7 fl oz water
85 g/3 oz butter
85 g/3 oz caster sugar
1 tbsp golden syrup
3 tbsp milk
1 tsp vanilla essence
1 tsp bicarbonate of soda
225 g/8 oz plain flour
2 tbsp cocoa powder

ICING
50 g/1¾ oz plain chocolate
4 tbsp water
50 g/1¾ oz butter
50 g/1¾ oz white chocolate
350 g/12 oz icing sugar

TO DECORATE
100 g/3½ oz plain chocolate shavings
100 g/3½ oz white chocolate shavings

Chocolate Chip Cupcakes

MAKES 8

Preheat the oven to 190°C/375°F/Gas Mark 5. Put 8 muffin paper cases in a muffin tray.

Put the margarine, sugar, eggs and flour in a large bowl and, using an electric hand whisk, beat together until just smooth. Fold in the chocolate chips. Spoon the mixture into the paper cases.

Bake the cupcakes in the preheated oven for 20–25 minutes, or until well risen and golden brown. Transfer to a wire rack to cool.

100 g/3½ oz soft tub margarine
100 g/3½ oz caster sugar
2 large eggs
100 g/3½ oz self-raising flour
100 g/3½ oz plain chocolate
    chips

Chocolate Cupcakes with Cream Cheese Icing

MAKES 18

Preheat the oven to 200°C/400°F/Gas Mark 6. Put 18 paper baking cases in 2 bun trays, or put 18 double-layer paper cases on a baking tray.

Put the butter and sugar in a bowl and beat together until light and fluffy. Gradually add the eggs, beating well after each addition. Add the milk, then fold in the chocolate chips. Sift in the flour and cocoa powder together, then fold into the mixture. Spoon the mixture into the paper cases and smooth the tops.

Bake the cupcakes in the preheated oven for 20 minutes, or until well risen and springy to the touch. Transfer to a wire rack and leave to cool.

To make the icing, break the chocolate into a small heatproof bowl and set the bowl over a saucepan of gently simmering water until melted. Leave to cool slightly. Put the cream cheese in a bowl and beat until softened, then beat in the slightly cooled chocolate.

Spread a little of the icing over the top of each cupcake, then leave to chill in the refrigerator for 1 hour before serving. Serve decorated with the chocolate curls.

85 g/3 oz butter, softened, or
  soft tub margarine
100 g/3½ oz caster sugar
2 eggs, lightly beaten
2 tbsp milk
55 g/2 oz plain chocolate chips
225 g/8 oz self-raising flour
25 g/1 oz cocoa powder

ICING
225 g/8 oz white chocolate
150 g/5½ oz low-fat cream
  cheese
chocolate curls, to decorate

Warm Molten-centred Chocolate Cupcakes

MAKES 8

Preheat the oven to 190°C/375°F/Gas Mark 5. Put 8 paper baking cases in a bun tray, or put 8 double-layer paper cases on a baking tray.

Put the margarine, sugar, egg, flour and cocoa powder in a large bowl and, using an electric hand whisk, beat together until just smooth.

Spoon half of the mixture into the paper cases. Using a teaspoon, make an indentation in the centre of each cake. Break the chocolate evenly into 8 squares and place a piece on top of each indentation, then spoon the remaining cake mixture on top.

Bake the cupcakes in the preheated oven for 20 minutes, or until well risen and springy to the touch. Leave the cupcakes for 2–3 minutes before serving warm, dusted with sifted icing sugar.

55 g/2 oz soft tub margarine
55 g/2 oz caster sugar
1 large egg
85 g/3 oz self-raising flour
1 tbsp cocoa powder
55 g/2 oz plain chocolate
icing sugar, sifted, for dusting

Devil's Food Cakes with Chocolate Icing

MAKES 18

Preheat the oven to 180°C/350°F/Gas Mark 4. Put 18 paper baking cases in a bun tray, or put 18 double-layer paper cases on a baking tray.

Put the margarine, sugar, eggs, flour, bicarbonate of soda and cocoa powder in a large bowl and, using an electric hand whisk, beat together until just smooth. Using a metal spoon, fold in the soured cream. Spoon the mixture into the paper cases.

Bake the cupcakes in the preheated oven for 20 minutes, or until well risen and firm to the touch. Transfer to a wire rack to cool.

To make the icing, break the chocolate into a heatproof bowl. Set the bowl over a saucepan of gently simmering water and heat until melted, stirring occasionally. Remove from the heat and allow to cool slightly, then whisk in the sugar and soured cream until combined. Spread the icing over the tops of the cupcakes and leave to set in the refrigerator before serving. Serve decorated with chocolate caraque.

50 g/1¾ oz soft tub margarine
115 g/4 oz soft dark brown sugar
2 large eggs
115 g/4 oz plain flour
½ tsp bicarbonate of soda
25 g/1 oz cocoa powder
125 ml/4 fl oz soured cream

ICING
125 g/4½ oz plain chocolate
2 tbsp caster sugar
150 ml/5 fl oz soured cream
chocolate caraque, to decorate

Mocha Cupcakes with Whipped Cream

MAKES 20

Preheat the oven to 180°C/350°F/Gas Mark 4. Put 20 paper baking cases in 2 bun trays, or put 20 double-layer paper cases on 2 baking trays.

Put the coffee powder, butter, sugar, honey and water in a saucepan and heat gently, stirring, until the sugar has dissolved. Bring to the boil, then reduce the heat and simmer for 5 minutes. Pour into a large heatproof bowl and leave to cool.

When the mixture has cooled, sift in the flour and cocoa powder. Dissolve the bicarbonate of soda in the milk, then add to the mixture with the egg and beat together until smooth. Spoon the mixture into the paper cases.

Bake the cupcakes in the preheated oven for 15–20 minutes, or until well risen and firm to the touch. Transfer to a wire rack to cool.

For the topping, whisk the cream in a bowl until it holds its shape. Just before serving, spoon heaped teaspoonfuls of cream on top of each cake, then dust lightly with sifted cocoa powder. You can store the cupcakes, without the topping, in the refrigerator until ready to serve.

2 tbsp instant espresso coffee powder
85 g/3 oz butter
85 g/3 oz caster sugar
1 tbsp clear honey
200 ml/7 fl oz water
225 g/8 oz plain flour
2 tbsp cocoa powder
1 tsp bicarbonate of soda
3 tbsp milk
1 large egg, lightly beaten

TOPPING
225 ml/8 fl oz whipping cream
cocoa powder, sifted, for dusting

Tiny Chocolate Cupcakes with Ganache Icing

MAKES 20

Preheat the oven to 190°C/375°F/Gas Mark 5. Put 20 double-layer mini paper cases on 2 baking trays.

Put the butter and sugar in a bowl and beat together until light and fluffy. Gradually beat in the egg. Sift in the flour and cocoa powder and then, using a metal spoon, fold them into the mixture. Stir in the milk.

Fill a piping bag, fitted with a large plain nozzle, with the mixture and pipe it into the paper cases, filling each one until half full.

Bake the cakes in the preheated oven for 10–15 minutes, or until well risen and firm to the touch. Transfer to a wire rack to cool.

To make the icing, break the chocolate into a saucepan and add the cream. Heat gently, stirring all the time, until the chocolate has melted. Pour into a large heatproof bowl and, using an electric hand whisk, beat the mixture for 10 minutes, or until thick, glossy and cool.

Fill a piping bag, fitted with a large star nozzle, with the icing and pipe a swirl on top of each cupcake. Alternatively, spoon the icing over the top of each cupcake. Chill in the refrigerator for 1 hour before serving. Serve decorated with a chocolate-coated coffee bean, if desired.

55 g/2 oz butter, softened
55 g/2 oz caster sugar
1 large egg, lightly beaten
55 g/2 oz self-raising flour
2 tbsp cocoa powder
1 tbsp milk
20 chocolate-coated coffee
   beans, to decorate (optional)

ICIING
100 g/3$\frac{1}{2}$ oz plain chocolate
100 ml/3$\frac{1}{2}$ fl oz double cream

Crumbly Cookies & Heavenly Bites

Chocolate Chip Cookies

MAKES 20

Preheat the oven to 180°C/350°F/Gas Mark 4. Grease 2 large baking sheets. Place the butter and sugar in a bowl and beat together with a wooden spoon until light and fluffy.

Beat in the egg, then add the oats, milk and vanilla essence. Beat together until well blended. Sift the flour, cocoa and baking powder into the mixture and stir. Stir in the chocolate pieces.

Place dessertspoonfuls of the mixture on the prepared baking sheets and flatten slightly with a fork. Bake in the preheated oven for 15 minutes, or until slightly risen and firm. Remove from the oven, cool on the baking sheets for 2 minutes, then transfer to wire racks to cool completely.

115 g/4 oz butter, softened, plus extra for greasing

115 g/4 oz light muscovado sugar

1 egg

100 g/3½ oz porridge oats

1 tbsp milk

1 tsp vanilla essence

125 g/4½ oz plain flour

1 tbsp cocoa powder

½ tsp baking powder

175 g/6 oz plain chocolate, broken into pieces

175 g/6 oz milk chocolate, broken into pieces

Double Chocolate Chip Cookies

MAKES 24

Preheat the oven to 180°C/350°F/Gas Mark 4. Grease 2 baking sheets with butter. Place the butter, sugar and vanilla essence in a large bowl and beat together. Gradually beat in the egg until the mixture is light and fluffy.

Sift the flour, salt and bicarbonate of soda over the mixture and fold in. Fold in the chocolate chips.

Drop heaped teaspoonfuls of the mixture on to the prepared baking sheets, allowing room for the cookies to spread during cooking. Bake in the preheated oven for 10–12 minutes, or until crisp outside but still soft inside. Leave to cool on the baking sheets for 2 minutes, then transfer to wire racks to cool completely.

200 g/7 oz butter, softened, plus
   extra for greasing
200 g/7 oz caster sugar
$\frac{1}{2}$ tsp vanilla essence
1 large egg
225 g/8 oz plain flour
pinch of salt
1 tsp bicarbonate of soda
115 g/4 oz white chocolate chips
115 g/4 oz plain chocolate chips

Zebra Cookies

MAKES 18–20

Melt the chocolate in a heatproof bowl set over a saucepan of gently simmering water. Leave to cool. Sift the flour and baking powder together.

Meanwhile, in a large bowl, whisk the egg, sugar, oil and vanilla essence together. Whisk in the cooled, melted chocolate until well blended, then gradually stir in the sifted flour. Cover the bowl and leave to chill for at least 3 hours.

Preheat the oven to 190°C/375°F/Gas Mark 5. Oil 1–2 large baking sheets. Using your hands, shape tablespoonfuls of the mixture into log shapes, each measuring about 5 cm/2 inches.

Roll the logs generously in the icing sugar, then place on the prepared baking sheets, allowing room for the biscuits to spread during cooking.

Bake the biscuits in the preheated oven for about 15 minutes, until firm. As soon as the biscuits are done, place 3 chocolate buttons down the centre of each, alternating the colours. Transfer to a wire rack and leave to cool.

55 g/2 oz plain chocolate, broken into pieces
140 g/5 oz plain flour
1 tsp baking powder
1 egg
140 g/5 oz caster sugar
50 ml/2 fl oz sunflower oil, plus extra for oiling
½ tsp vanilla essence
2 tbsp icing sugar
1 small packet milk chocolate buttons
1 small packet white chocolate buttons

Chocolate Orange Cookies

MAKES 30

Preheat the oven to 180°C/350°F/Gas Mark 4. Line 2 baking sheets with sheets of greaseproof paper.

Beat together the butter and sugar until the mixture is light and fluffy. Beat in the egg and milk until well combined. Sift the flour and cocoa into the bowl and gradually mix together to form a soft dough. Use your fingers to incorporate the last of the flour and bring the dough together.

Roll out the dough on a lightly floured work surface until 5 mm/^{1}/$_4$ inch thick. Cut out circles using a 5-cm/2-inch fluted round biscuit cutter.

Place the circles on the prepared baking sheets and bake in the preheated oven for 10–12 minutes, or until golden.

Let the biscuits cool on the baking sheet for a few minutes before transferring them to a wire rack to cool completely and become crisp.

To make the icing, put the icing sugar in a bowl and stir in enough orange juice to form a thin icing that will coat the back of the spoon. Put a spoonful of icing in the centre of each biscuit and leave to set. Place the plain chocolate in a heatproof bowl set over a saucepan of gently simmering water and stir until melted. Drizzle thin lines of melted chocolate over the biscuits and leave to set before serving.

90 g/3^1/$_4$ oz butter, softened

60 g/2^1/$_4$ oz caster sugar

1 egg

1 tbsp milk

280 g/10 oz plain flour, plus extra
   for dusting

2 tbsp cocoa powder

ICING

175 g/6 oz icing sugar, sifted

3 tbsp orange juice

a little plain chocolate, broken
   into pieces

Nutty Drizzles

MAKES 24

Preheat the oven to 180°C/350°F/Gas Mark 4. Grease a couple of large baking sheets. In a large bowl, cream together the butter, sugar and egg. Add the flour, baking powder, bicarbonate of soda, oats, bran and wheatgerm and mix together until well combined. Finally, stir in the nuts, chocolate chips and dried fruit.

Put 24 rounded tablespoonfuls of the mixture on to the greased baking sheets. Transfer to the preheated oven and bake for 12 minutes, or until the biscuits are golden brown.

Remove the biscuits from the oven, then transfer to a wire rack and leave to cool. Meanwhile, put the chocolate pieces in a heatproof bowl set over a saucepan of gently simmering water until melted. Stir the chocolate, then leave to cool slightly. Use a spoon to drizzle the chocolate in waves over the biscuits, or spoon it into a piping bag and pipe zig-zag lines over the biscuits. Store in an airtight container in the refrigerator before serving.

200 g/7 oz butter or margarine, plus extra for greasing
275 g/9$\frac{1}{2}$ oz Demerara sugar
1 egg
140 g/5 oz plain flour, sifted
1 tsp baking powder
1 tsp bicarbonate of soda
125 g/4$\frac{1}{2}$ oz rolled oats
1 tbsp bran
1 tbsp wheatgerm
115 g/4 oz mixed nuts, toasted and roughly chopped
200 g/7 oz plain chocolate chips
115 g/4 oz mixed raisins and sultanas
175 g/6 oz plain chocolate, roughly chopped

Cookies & Cream Sandwiches

SERVES 4

Preheat the oven to 160°C/325°F/Gas Mark 3. Line a greaseproof sheet with non-stick baking paper. Place the butter and sugar in a large bowl and beat together until light and fluffy. Sift the flour, cocoa and ground cinnamon into the bowl and mix to form a dough.

Place the dough between 2 sheets of non-stick baking paper and roll out to 3-mm/^{1}/8-inch thick. Cut out 6-cm/2^1/2-inch circles and place on the prepared baking sheet. Bake in the preheated oven for 15 minutes, or until firm to the touch. Leave to cool for 2 minutes, then transfer to wire racks to cool completely.

Meanwhile, make the filling. Place the chocolate and cream in a saucepan and heat gently until the chocolate has melted. Stir until smooth. Leave to cool, then leave to chill in the refrigerator for 2 hours, or until firm. Sandwich the biscuits together in pairs with a spoonful of chocolate cream and serve.

125 g/4^1/2 oz butter, softened
75 g/2^3/4 oz icing sugar
115 g/4 oz plain flour
40 g/1^1/2 oz cocoa powder
^{1}/2 tsp ground cinnamon

FILLING
125 g/4^1/2 oz plain chocolate,
  broken into pieces
50 ml/2 fl oz double cream

White Chocolate Cookies

MAKES 24

Preheat the oven to 190°C/375°F/Gas Mark 5. Grease several baking sheets lightly with a little butter.

In a large mixing bowl, cream together the butter and sugar until light and fluffy.

Gradually add the beaten egg to the creamed mixture, beating well after each addition.

Sift the flour and salt into the creamed mixture and blend well.

Stir in the white chocolate chunks and the chopped Brazil nuts.

Place heaped teaspoonfuls of the mixture on the prepared baking sheets. Put no more than 6 on each sheet because the cookies will spread during cooking.

Bake in the oven for 10–12 minutes, or until just golden brown.

Transfer the cookies to wire racks and leave until completely cold.

115 g/4 oz butter, softened, plus extra for greasing
115 g/4 oz soft brown sugar
1 egg, beaten
250 g/9 oz self-raising flour
pinch of salt
125 g/4$\frac{1}{2}$ oz white chocolate, chopped
50 g/1$\frac{3}{4}$ oz chopped Brazil nuts

Chocolate & Coffee Wholemeal Cookies

MAKES 24

Preheat the oven to 190°C/375°F/Gas Mark 5. Grease 2 large baking sheets. Cream the butter and sugar together in a bowl. Add the egg and beat well, using a hand whisk if preferred.

In a separate bowl, sift together the plain flour, bicarbonate of soda and salt, then add in the wholemeal flour and bran. Mix in the egg mixture, then stir in the chocolate chips, oats, coffee and hazelnuts. Mix well, with an electric whisk if preferred.

Put 24 rounded tablespoonfuls of the mixture on to the prepared baking sheets, allowing room for the biscuits to spread during cooking. Alternatively, with lightly floured hands, break off pieces of the mixture and roll into balls (about 25 g/1 oz each), place on the baking sheets and flatten them with the back of a teaspoon.

Transfer the baking sheets to the preheated oven and bake for 16–18 minutes, or until the biscuits are golden brown.

Remove from the oven, transfer the biscuits to a wire rack and leave to cool before serving.

175 g/6 oz butter or margarine, plus extra for greasing
200 g/7 oz soft brown sugar
1 egg
70 g/2½ oz plain flour
1 tsp bicarbonate of soda
pinch of salt
70 g/2½ oz wholemeal flour
1 tbsp bran
225 g/8 oz plain chocolate chips
185 g/6½ oz rolled oats
1 tbsp strong coffee
100 g/3½ oz hazelnuts, toasted and roughly chopped

Mocha Walnut Cookies

MAKES ABOUT 16

Preheat the oven to 180°C/350°F/Gas Mark 4. Grease 2 baking sheets. Put the butter, light muscovado sugar and caster sugar in a bowl and beat until light and fluffy. Put the vanilla essence, coffee and egg in a separate bowl and whisk together.

Gradually add the coffee mixture to the butter and sugar, beating until fluffy. Sift the flour, baking powder and bicarbonate of soda into the mixture and fold in carefully. Fold in the chocolate chips and walnuts.

Spoon heaped teaspoonfuls of the mixture on to the prepared baking sheets, allowing room for the cookies to spread. Bake for 10–15 minutes, until crisp on the outside but still soft inside. Leave to cool on the sheets for 2 minutes, then transfer to wire racks to cool completely.

115 g/4 oz butter, softened, plus extra for greasing

115 g/4 oz light muscovado sugar

85 g/3 oz caster sugar

1 tsp vanilla essence

1 tbsp instant coffee granules, dissolved in 1 tbsp hot water

1 egg

175 g/6 oz plain flour

½ tsp baking powder

¼ tsp bicarbonate of soda

55 g/2 oz milk chocolate chips

55 g/2 oz walnuts, roughly chopped

Chocolate Peanut Butter Slices

MAKES 26

Preheat the oven to 180°C/350°F/Gas Mark 4. Finely chop the chocolate. Sift the flour and baking powder into a large bowl.

Add the butter to the flour and rub in until the mixture resembles breadcrumbs. Stir in the sugar, oats and chopped nuts.

Put a quarter of the mixture into a bowl and stir in the chopped chocolate. Set aside.

Stir the egg into the remaining mixture, then press into the bottom of a 30 x 20-cm/12 x 8-inch roasting tin.

Bake the base in the preheated oven for 15 minutes. Meanwhile, mix the condensed milk and peanut butter together. Pour the mixture over the base and spread evenly, then sprinkle the reserved chocolate mixture on top and press down lightly.

Return to the oven and bake for an additional 20 minutes, until golden brown. Leave to cool in the tin, then cut into slices.

300 g/10½ oz milk chocolate
350 g/12 oz plain flour
1 tsp baking powder
225 g/8 oz butter
350 g/12 oz soft brown sugar
175 g/6 oz rolled oats
70 g/2½ oz chopped mixed nuts
1 egg, beaten
400 ml/14 fl oz condensed milk
70 g/2½ oz crunchy peanut
   butter

Chocolate Wheatmeals

MAKES 20

Preheat the oven to 180°C/350°F/Gas Mark 4. Lightly grease a baking sheet. Beat the butter and sugar until fluffy. Add the egg and beat well. Stir in the wheatgerm and flours. Bring the mixture together with your hands.

Roll rounded teaspoonfuls of the mixture into balls and place on the prepared baking sheet, allowing room for the biscuits to spread during cooking.

Flatten the biscuits slightly with the tines of a fork. Bake in the preheated oven for 15–20 minutes, until golden. Leave to cool on the baking sheet for a few minutes before transferring to a wire rack to cool completely.

Put the chocolate in a heatproof bowl set over a saucepan of gently simmering water until melted. Dip each biscuit in the chocolate to cover the flat side and a little way around the edges. Let the excess drip back into the bowl.

Place the biscuits on a sheet of greaseproof paper in a cool place and leave the chocolate to set before serving.

75 g/2¾ oz butter, plus extra for greasing
125 g/4½ oz Demerara sugar
1 egg
1 tbsp wheatgerm
150 g/5½ oz wholewheat self-raising flour
70 g/2½ oz self-raising flour, sifted
125 g/4½ oz chocolate, broken into pieces

Chocolate Temptations

MAKES 24

Preheat the oven to 180°C/350°F/Gas Mark 4. Grease a large baking sheet. Put 225 g/8 oz of the plain chocolate with the butter and coffee into a heatproof bowl set over a saucepan of gently simmering water and heat until the chocolate is almost melted.

Meanwhile, beat the eggs in a bowl until fluffy. Whisk in the sugar gradually until thick. Remove the chocolate from the heat and stir until smooth. Add to the egg mixture and stir until combined.

Sift the flour, baking powder and salt into a bowl and stir into the chocolate mixture. Chop 85 g/3 oz of the plain chocolate into pieces and stir into the mixture. Stir in the almond essence and chopped nuts.

Put 24 tablespoonfuls of the mixture on to the baking sheet, transfer to the preheated oven and bake for 16 minutes. Transfer the biscuits to a wire rack to cool. To decorate, melt the remaining chocolate (plain and white) in turn as earlier, then spoon into a piping bag and pipe lines on to the biscuits.

90 g/3¼ oz butter, plus extra
  for greasing
365 g/12½ oz plain chocolate
1 tsp strong coffee
2 eggs
140 g/5 oz soft brown sugar
185 g/6½ oz plain flour
¼ tsp baking powder
pinch of salt
2 tsp almond essence
85 g/3 oz Brazil nuts, chopped
85 g/3 oz hazelnuts, chopped
40 g/1½ oz white chocolate

Chocolate Scones

MAKES 9

Preheat the oven to 220°C/425°F/Gas Mark 7. Lightly grease a baking sheet. Place the flour in a mixing bowl. Cut the butter into small pieces and rub it into the flour with your fingertips until the scone mixture resembles fine breadcrumbs.

Stir in the caster sugar and chocolate chips. Mix in enough of the milk to form a soft dough.

On a work surface, lightly dusted with flour, roll out the dough to form a 10 x 15-cm/4 x 6-inch rectangle, about 2.5 cm/1 inch thick. Cut the dough into 9 rectangles.

Place the scones, spaced well apart, on the prepared baking sheet. Brush the tops with a little milk and bake in the preheated oven for 10–12 minutes, until risen and golden.

70 g/2$\frac{1}{2}$ oz butter,
 plus extra for greasing
280 g/10 oz self-raising flour,
 sifted
1 tbsp caster sugar
55 g/2 oz chocolate chips
150 ml/5 fl oz milk
plain flour, for dusting

Chocolate Pistachio Bars

MAKES 24

Preheat the oven to 160°C/325°F/Gas Mark 3. Grease a baking sheet with butter. Put the chocolate and the butter in a heatproof bowl set over a saucepan of gently simmering water. Stir over a low heat until melted and smooth. Remove from the heat and cool slightly.

Sift the flour and baking powder into a bowl and mix in the caster sugar, cornmeal, lemon rind, amaretto, egg and pistachio nuts. Stir in the chocolate mixture and mix to a soft dough.

Lightly dust your hands with flour, divide the dough in half and shape each piece into a 28-cm/11-inch long cylinder. Transfer the cylinders to the prepared baking sheet and flatten, with the palm of your hand, to about 2 cm/³/4 inch thick. Bake in the preheated oven for about 20 minutes, until firm to the touch.

Remove the baking sheet from the oven and leave the cooked pieces to cool. When cool, put the cooked pieces on a chopping board and slice them diagonally into thin biscuits. Return them to the baking sheet and bake for an additional 10 minutes, until crisp. Remove from the oven and transfer to a wire rack to cool. Dust lightly with icing sugar.

2 tbsp butter, plus extra for greasing
175 g/6 oz plain chocolate, broken into pieces
350 g/12 oz self-raising flour, plus extra for dusting
1½ tsp baking powder
85 g/3 oz caster sugar
70 g/2½ oz cornmeal
finely grated rind of 1 lemon
2 tsp amaretto
1 egg, lightly beaten
115 g/4 oz pistachio nuts, roughly chopped
2 tbsp icing sugar, for dusting

Chocolate Caramel Squares

MAKES 16

Preheat the oven to 180°C/350°F/Gas Mark 4. Beat together the margarine and brown sugar in a bowl until light and fluffy. Beat in the flour and the rolled oats. Use your fingertips to bring the mixture together, if necessary.

Press the mixture into the base of a greased 20-cm/8-inch square, shallow cake tin.

Bake the mixture in the preheated oven for 25 minutes, or until just golden and firm. Cool in the tin.

Place the ingredients for the caramel filling in a saucepan and heat gently, stirring until the sugar has dissolved. Bring slowly to the boil over a very low heat, then boil very gently for 3–4 minutes, stirring constantly, until thickened.

Pour the caramel filling over the oat layer in the tin and leave to set.

Melt the plain chocolate and spread it over the caramel. If using the white chocolate, place in a heatproof bowl set over a saucepan of gently simmering water until melted. Pipe lines of white chocolate over the plain chocolate. Using a cocktail stick, feather the white chocolate into the plain chocolate. Leave to set, then cut into squares to serve.

75 g/2¾ oz margarine, plus
   extra for greasing
60 g/2¼ oz soft brown sugar
140 g/5 oz plain flour
40 g/1½ oz rolled oats

CARAMEL FILLING
2 tbsp butter
2 tbsp soft brown sugar
225 ml/8 fl oz condensed milk

TOPPING
100 g/3½ oz plain chocolate
25 g/1 oz white chocolate
   (optional)

Chocolate Chip Flapjacks

MAKES 12

Preheat the oven to 180°C/350°F/Gas Mark 4. Lightly grease a 20-cm/8-inch square, shallow cake tin.

Place the butter, caster sugar and golden syrup in a saucepan and cook over a low heat, stirring constantly, until the butter and sugar melt and the mixture is well combined.

Remove the saucepan from the heat and stir in the rolled oats until they are well coated. Add the chocolate chips and the sultanas and mix well to combine everything.

Turn into the prepared tin and press down well.

Bake in the preheated oven for 30 minutes. Cool slightly, then mark into squares. When almost cold, cut into squares and transfer to a wire rack to cool completely.

115 g/4 oz butter, plus extra for greasing
60 g/2¼ oz caster sugar
1 tbsp golden syrup
350 g/12 oz rolled oats
85 g/3 oz plain chocolate chips
85 g/3 oz sultanas

Ladies' Kisses

MAKES 20

Line 3 baking sheets with greaseproof paper, or use 3 non-stick sheets. Cream the butter and sugar together until pale and fluffy. Beat in the egg yolk, then beat in the almonds and flour. Continue beating until thoroughly mixed. Shape the dough into a ball, wrap in clingfilm and chill in the refrigerator for 1½–2 hours.

Preheat the oven to 160°C/325°F/Gas Mark 3. Unwrap the dough, break off walnut-sized pieces and roll them into balls between the palms of your hands. Place the dough balls on the prepared baking sheets, allowing space for the biscuits to spread during cooking. You may need to cook them in batches. Bake in the preheated oven for 20–25 minutes, until golden. Carefully transfer the biscuits on to wire racks, to cool.

Melt the chocolate in a heatproof bowl set over a saucepan of gently simmering water. Spread the melted chocolate on the flat sides of the cookies and sandwich them together in pairs. Return to the wire racks to cool.

175 g/6 oz butter
115 g/4 oz caster sugar
1 egg yolk
100 g/3½ oz ground almonds
175 g/6 oz plain flour
55 g/2 oz plain chocolate, broken into pieces

Cool Chocolate

Chocolate Chip Ice Cream with Hot Chocolate Fudge Sauce

SERVES 4–6

Pour the milk into a heavy-based saucepan, add the vanilla pod and bring almost to the boil. Remove from the heat and leave to infuse for 30 minutes. Meanwhile, chop the chocolate into small pieces and set aside.

Put the sugar and egg yolks in a large bowl and whisk together until pale and the mixture leaves a trail when the whisk is lifted. Remove the vanilla pod from the milk, then slowly add the milk to the sugar mixture, stirring all the time with a wooden spoon. Strain the mixture into the rinsed-out saucepan or a double boiler and cook over a low heat for 10–15 minutes, stirring all the time, until the mixture thickens enough to coat the back of the spoon. Do not boil or it will curdle.

Remove the custard from the heat and leave to cool for at least 1 hour, stirring from time to time to prevent a skin from forming. Meanwhile, whip the cream until it holds its shape. Keep in the refrigerator until ready to use.

If using an ice cream machine, fold the cold custard into the whipped cream, then churn the mixture in the machine following the manufacturer's instructions. Just before the ice cream freezes, add the chocolate pieces. Alternatively, freeze the custard in a freezerproof container, uncovered, for 1–2 hours, or until it begins to set around the edges. Turn the custard into a bowl and stir with a fork or beat in a food processor until smooth. Fold in the whipped cream and chocolate pieces. Return to the freezer and freeze for a further 2–3 hours, or until firm or required. Cover the container with a lid for storing.

Make the chocolate sauce just before you serve the ice cream. Put the chocolate, butter and milk in a heatproof bowl set over a saucepan of simmering water and heat gently, stirring occasionally, until the chocolate has melted and the sauce is smooth. Transfer the mixture to a heavy-based saucepan and stir in the sugar and syrup. Heat gently until the sugar has dissolved, then bring to the boil and boil, without stirring, for 5 minutes.

Serve the hot sauce poured over the ice cream.

300 ml/10 fl oz full-fat milk
1 vanilla pod
115 g/4 oz milk chocolate
85 g/3 oz caster sugar
3 egg yolks
300 ml/10 fl oz whipping cream

CHOCOLATE FUDGE SAUCE
50 g/1¾ oz milk chocolate, broken into pieces
25 g/1 oz butter
4 tbsp full-fat milk
225 g/8 oz soft light brown sugar
2 tbsp golden syrup

Chocolate Praline Ice Cream

SERVES 4–6

To prepare the praline, brush a baking tray with oil. Put the sugar, water and nuts in a large heavy-based saucepan and heat gently, stirring, until the sugar has dissolved, then let the mixture bubble gently for 6–10 minutes, or until lightly golden brown. Do not stir the mixture while it is bubbling and ensure that it does not burn.

As soon as the mixture has turned golden brown, immediately pour it on to the prepared baking tray and spread it out evenly. Leave to cool for 1 hour, or until cold and hardened. When the praline has hardened, finely crush it in a food processor or place it in a polythene bag and crush with a hard object.

To prepare the ice cream, put the chocolate and milk in a saucepan and heat gently, stirring, until the chocolate has melted and the mixture is smooth. Remove from the heat.

Put the sugar and egg yolks in a large bowl and whisk together until pale and the mixture leaves a trail when the whisk is lifted. Slowly add the milk mixture, stirring all the time with a wooden spoon. Strain the mixture into the rinsed-out saucepan or a double boiler and cook over a low heat for 10–15 minutes, stirring all the time, until the mixture thickens enough to coat the back of the spoon. Do not allow the mixture to boil or it will curdle.

Remove the custard from the heat and leave to cool for at least 1 hour, stirring from time to time to prevent a skin from forming. Meanwhile, whip the cream until it holds its shape. Keep in the refrigerator until ready to use.

If using an ice cream machine, fold the cold custard into the whipped cream, then churn the mixture in the machine following the manufacturer's instructions. Just before the ice cream freezes, add the praline. Alternatively, freeze the custard in a freezerproof container, uncovered, for 1–2 hours, or until it begins to set around the edges. Turn the custard into a bowl and stir with a fork or beat in a food processor until smooth. Fold in the whipped cream and praline. Return to the freezer and freeze for a further 2–3 hours, or until firm or required. Cover the container with a lid for storing.

85 g/3 oz plain dark chocolate, broken into pieces
300 ml/10 fl oz full-fat milk
85 g/3 oz caster sugar
3 egg yolks
300 ml/10 fl oz whipping cream

PRALINE
vegetable oil, for oiling
100 g/3½ oz granulated sugar
2 tbsp water
50 g/1¾ oz blanched almonds

White & Dark Chocolate Ice Cream

SERVES 4

Put the egg yolks and sugar into a large, heatproof bowl and beat until fluffy. Heat the milk, cream and dark chocolate in a saucepan over a low heat, stirring, until melted and almost boiling. Remove from the heat and whisk into the egg mixture. Return to the pan and cook, stirring, over a low heat until thick. Do not let it simmer. Transfer to a heatproof bowl and leave to cool. Cover the bowl with clingfilm and chill for 1^1/$_2$ hours. Remove from the refrigerator and stir in the white chocolate.

Transfer to a freezerproof container and freeze for 1 hour. Remove from the freezer, transfer to a bowl and whisk to break up the ice crystals. Return to the container and freeze for 30 minutes. Repeat twice more, freezing for 30 minutes and whisking each time. Alternatively, transfer the mixture to an ice-cream machine and process for 15 minutes.

Scoop into serving bowls, decorate with mint leaves and serve.

6 egg yolks
100 g/3^1/$_2$ oz caster sugar
350 ml/12 fl oz milk
175 ml/6 fl oz double cream
100 g/3^1/$_2$ oz dark chocolate, chopped
75 g/2^3/$_4$ oz white chocolate, grated or finely chopped
fresh mint leaves, to decorate

Chocolate Peppermint Crisp Terrine

SERVES 6–8

Line a 450-g/1-lb loaf tin or 850-ml/1½-pint oblong freezerproof plastic container with greaseproof paper, allowing it to hang over the edges of the container so that the ice cream can be easily removed. Pour the single cream into a heavy-based saucepan and bring almost to the boil. Remove from the heat and stir in the peppermint essence.

Put the egg yolks and sugar in a large bowl and whisk together until pale and the mixture leaves a trail when the whisk is lifted. Slowly add the cream, stirring all the time with a wooden spoon.

Strain the mixture into the rinsed-out saucepan or a double boiler and cook over a low heat for 10–15 minutes, stirring all the time, until the mixture thickens enough to coat the back of the spoon. Do not allow the mixture to boil or it will curdle. Remove the custard the heat and leave to cool for at least 1 hour, stirring from time to time to prevent a skin from forming.

Meanwhile, put the peppermint crisps, a few at a time, into a food processor and chop into small pieces. Alternatively, chop the peppermint crisps into small pieces by hand.

Whip the double cream until it just holds its shape. When the custard is cold, stir in the peppermint crisp pieces, then fold in the whipped cream until well blended.

Turn the mixture into the prepared tin or plastic container and then freeze, uncovered, for 4 hours, or until firm or required. Cover the container with a lid for storing.

To serve the ice cream, uncover, stand the tin or plastic container in hot water for a few seconds to loosen it, then invert it on to a serving dish. Remove the greaseproof paper and, using a hot knife, cut the terrine into slices. Serve decorated with chocolate shapes.

300 ml/10 fl oz single cream
½ tsp peppermint essence
4 egg yolks
115 g/4 oz caster sugar
200 g/7 oz plain dark chocolate peppermint crisps
300 ml/10 fl oz double cream
chocolate shapes, to decorate

Chocolate Ice Cream Roll

SERVES 8

Line a 38 x 25-cm/15 x 10-inch Swiss roll tin with greaseproof paper. Grease the bottom and dust with flour. Put the eggs and caster sugar in a heatproof bowl set over a saucepan of simmering water. Whisk over a low heat for 5–10 minutes until the mixture is pale and fluffy. Remove from the heat and continue whisking for 10 minutes until the mixture is cool and the whisk leaves a ribbon trail when lifted. Sift the flour and cocoa powder over the surface and fold them in, gently.

Preheat the oven to 190°C/375°F/Gas Mark 5. Pour the mixture into the prepared tin and spread out evenly with a spatula. Bake in the preheated oven for 15 minutes, until firm to the touch and starting to shrink from the sides of the tin.

Spread out a clean cloth and cover with a sheet of greaseproof paper. Lightly dust with icing sugar. Turn out the cake on to the greaseproof paper and carefully peel off the lining paper. Trim off any crusty edges. Starting from a short side, pick up the cake and the greaseproof paper and roll them up together. Wrap the cloth around the rolled cake and place on a wire rack to cool.

Remove the ice cream from the freezer and put it in the refrigerator for 15–20 minutes to soften slightly. Remove the cloth and unroll the cake. Remove the greaseproof paper and spread the ice cream evenly over the cake, then roll it up again, this time without the greaseproof paper. Wrap the cake in foil and place in the freezer.

Remove the cake from the freezer about 20 minutes before serving. Unwrap, place on a serving plate and dust with icing sugar. Arrange the chocolate caraque over the top. Place the cake in the refrigerator 15 minutes before serving to soften slightly.

butter, for greasing

115 g/4 oz plain flour, plus extra
  for dusting

4 eggs

115 g/4 oz caster sugar

3 tbsp cocoa powder

icing sugar, for dusting

600 g/1 lb 5 oz chocolate
  ice cream

marbled chocolate caraque,
  to decorate

Chocolate Ice Cream Bombe

SERVES 4

Put a 1.4-litre/2^1/$_2$-pint bombe mould into the freezer. Place the eggs, egg yolks and sugar in a heatproof bowl and beat together until well blended. Put the single cream and chocolate in a saucepan and heat gently until the chocolate has melted, then continue to heat, stirring until almost boiling. Pour on to the egg mixture, stirring vigorously, then place the bowl over a saucepan of simmering water, making sure that the bottom of the bowl does not touch the water. Cook, stirring, until the mixture coats the back of the spoon. Strain into another bowl and leave to cool. Place the double cream in a bowl and whisk until slightly thickened, then fold into the cooled chocolate mixture.

Freeze in an ice-cream maker, following the manufacturer's directions. Alternatively, pour the mixture into a freezerproof container, cover and freeze for 2 hours until just frozen. Spoon into a bowl and beat with a fork to break down the ice crystals. Return to the freezer until almost solid. Line the bombe mould with the chocolate ice cream and return to the freezer.

To make the white chocolate ice cream, put the chocolate and half the milk in a saucepan and heat gently until the chocolate has just melted. Remove from the heat and stir. Put the sugar and remaining milk in another saucepan and heat gently until the sugar has melted. Set aside to cool, then stir into the cooled chocolate mixture. Place the cream in a bowl and whisk until slightly thickened, then fold into the chocolate mixture. Spoon into the centre of the bombe, cover and freeze for about 4 hours, until firm. To serve, dip the mould briefly into warm water, then turn out on to a serving plate. Decorate with chocolate shapes.

PLAIN CHOCOLATE ICE CREAM

2 eggs

2 egg yolks

115 g/4 oz caster sugar

300 ml/10 fl oz single cream

225 g/8 oz plain chocolate, chopped

300 ml/10 fl oz double cream

WHITE CHOCOLATE ICE CREAM

140 g/5 oz white chocolate, broken into pieces

150 ml/5 fl oz milk

55 g/2 oz golden caster sugar

300 ml/10 fl oz double cream

chocolate shapes, to decorate

Chocolate Ice Cream Bites

SERVES 6

Line a baking tray with clingfilm.

Using a melon baller, scoop out balls of ice cream and place them on the prepared baking tray. Alternatively, cut the ice cream into bite-sized cubes. Stick a cocktail stick in each piece and return to the freezer until very hard.

Place the chocolate and the butter in a heatproof bowl set over a saucepan of gently simmering water until melted. Quickly dip the frozen ice cream balls or cubes into the warm chocolate and return to the freezer. Keep them there until ready to serve.

600 g/1 lb 5 oz good-quality
  ice cream
200 g/7 oz dark chocolate
2 tbsp unsalted butter

Rich Chocolate Mousses

MAKES 4

Break the chocolate into small pieces and put it in a heatproof bowl over a saucepan of gently simmering water. Add the caster sugar and butter and melt together, stirring, until smooth. Remove from the heat, stir in the brandy, and leave to cool a little. Add the egg yolks and beat until smooth.

In a separate bowl, whisk the egg whites until stiff peaks form, then fold them into the chocolate mixture. Place a stainless steel cooking ring on each of 4 small serving plates, then spoon the mixture into each ring and smooth the surfaces. Transfer to the refrigerator and chill for at least 4 hours until set.

Remove the mousses from the refrigerator and carefully remove the cooking rings. Dust with cocoa powder and serve immediately.

300 g/10$\frac{1}{2}$ oz plain chocolate
5 tbsp caster sugar
1$\frac{1}{2}$ tbsp unsalted butter
1 tbsp brandy
4 eggs, separated
cocoa powder, for dusting

Tiramisù Layers

MAKES 6

Whip the cream until it just holds its shape. Beat the mascarpone to soften slightly, then fold in the whipped cream. Melt the chocolate in a heatproof bowl set over a saucepan of simmering water, stirring occasionally. Let the chocolate cool slightly, then stir it into the mascarpone and cream mixture.

Mix the hot coffee and sugar in a saucepan and stir until dissolved. Leave to cool then add the dark rum. Dip the sponge finger biscuits into the mixture briefly so that they absorb some coffee and rum mixture but do not become soggy.

Place 3 sponge finger biscuits on each of 6 serving plates. Spoon a layer of the chocolate, mascarpone and cream mixture over the sponge finger biscuits.

Place 3 more sponge finger biscuits on top of the chocolate mixture on each plate. Spread another layer of chocolate mixture and place 3 more sponge finger biscuits on top.

Leave to chill in the refrigerator for at least 1 hour. Dust with a little cocoa powder just before serving.

150 ml/5 fl oz double cream
400 g/14 oz mascarpone cheese
300 g/10 oz plain chocolate
400 ml/14 fl oz hot black coffee
55 g/2 oz caster sugar
6 tbsp dark rum or brandy
54 sponge finger biscuits
cocoa powder, for dusting

White Chocolate Terrine

SERVES 8

Line a 450-g/1-lb loaf tin with foil or clingfilm pressing out as many creases as you can.

Place the granulated sugar and water in a heavy-based saucepan and heat gently, stirring until the sugar has dissolved. Bring to the boil and boil for 1–2 minutes until syrupy, then remove from the heat.

Break the white chocolate into small pieces and stir it into the hot syrup, continuing to stir until the chocolate has melted and combined with the syrup. Let the mixture cool slightly.

Beat the egg yolks into the chocolate mixture. Leave to cool completely.

Lightly whip the cream until it is just holding its shape, and fold it into the chocolate mixture.

Whisk the egg whites in a greasefree bowl until soft peaks form. Fold the whites into the chocolate mixture. Pour into the prepared loaf tin and freeze overnight.

To serve, remove the terrine from the freezer about 10–15 minutes before serving. Turn out of the tin and cut into slices. Serve with fruit coulis and strawberries.

2 tbsp granulated sugar
5 tbsp water
300 g/10½ oz white chocolate
3 eggs, separated
300 ml/10 fl oz double cream

TO SERVE
fruit coulis
fresh strawberries

Chocolate & Orange Slices

SERVES 8

Lightly grease a 450-g/1-lb loaf tin and line it with clingfilm. Put the chocolate in a heatproof bowl set over a saucepan of gently simmering water. Stir over a low heat until melted. Remove from the heat and leave to cool slightly.

Meanwhile, peel the oranges, removing all traces of pith. Cut the zest into very thin strips. Beat the egg yolks into the chocolate, one at a time, then add most of the orange zest (reserving the rest for decoration), and all the crème fraîche and raisins, and beat until thoroughly combined. Spoon the mixture into the prepared tin, cover with clingfilm and chill for 3–4 hours, until set.

To serve, remove the tin from the refrigerator and turn out the chocolate mould. Remove the clingfilm and cut the mould into slices. Place a slice on individual serving plates and add whipped cream to serve. Decorate with the remaining orange zest.

2 tsp butter, for greasing

450 g/1 lb plain chocolate,
  broken into pieces

3 small, loose-skinned oranges,
  such as tangerines, mandarins
  or satsumas

4 egg yolks

200 ml/7 fl oz crème fraîche

2 tbsp raisins

300 ml/10 fl oz whipped cream,
  to serve

Chocolate Hazelnut Parfaits

MAKES 6

Preheat the grill to medium. Spread out the hazelnuts on a baking tray and toast under the grill for about 5 minutes, shaking the sheet from time to time, until golden all over. Set aside to cool.

Put the chocolate in a heatproof bowl set over a saucepan of gently simmering water. Stir over a low heat until melted, then remove from the heat and cool. Put the toasted hazelnuts in a food processor and process until finely ground.

Whisk the cream until it is stiff, then fold in the ground hazelnuts and set aside. Add 3 tablespoons of the sugar to the egg yolks and beat for 10 minutes until pale and thick.

Whisk the egg whites in a separate bowl until soft peaks form. Whisk in the remaining sugar, a little at a time, until the whites are stiff and glossy. Stir the cooled chocolate into the egg yolk mixture, then fold in the cream and finally, fold in the egg whites. Divide the mixture among 6 freezerproof timbales or moulds, cover with clingfilm, and freeze for at least 8 hours, or overnight, until firm.

Transfer the frozen parfaits to the refrigerator about 10 minutes before serving to soften slightly. Turn out on to individual serving plates, dust the tops lightly with cocoa powder, decorate with mint sprigs and serve with wafer biscuits.

175 g/6 oz blanched hazelnuts
175 g/6 oz plain chocolate, broken into small pieces
600 ml/1 pint double cream
250 g/9 oz icing sugar
3 eggs, separated
1 tbsp cocoa powder, for dusting
6 small fresh mint sprigs, to decorate
wafer biscuits, to serve

Cherry & Chocolate Meringue

SERVES 4

Preheat the oven to 140°C/275°F/Gas Mark 1. Line a baking sheet with greaseproof paper.

Whisk the egg whites until stiff. Gradually add the sugar, and whisk until stiff and shiny. Fold in the cornflour, vinegar, cocoa and chocolate. Spread the meringue on to the baking sheet to form a 24-cm/9^1/2-inch disc. Bake for 1^1/2 hours.

Turn off the oven and leave the meringue in the oven for 45 minutes.

To make the topping, whisk the cream and icing sugar until stiff, then chill. Cut the cherries in half and remove the stones, but keep a few whole. Melt the maple syrup with the butter in a frying pan and stir in the stoned cherries to coat, then set aside to cool.

To serve, peel off the paper from the cool meringue and put the meringue on to a dish. Spoon the cream into the centre and pile on the cherries, using the whole ones around the edge. Top with the caraque.

4 large egg whites
200 g/7 oz caster sugar
1 tsp cornflour, sifted
1 tsp white wine vinegar
1 tbsp cocoa powder
140 g/5 oz plain chocolate,
    chopped

TOPPING
400 ml/14 fl oz double cream
25 g/1 oz icing sugar, sifted
450 g/1 lb black cherries
4 tbsp maple syrup
4 tbsp unsalted butter
plain chocolate caraque,
    to decorate

Deep Chocolate Cheesecake

SERVES 4–6

Grease a 20-cm/8-inch loose-bottomed cake tin.

To make the base, put the crushed biscuits, cocoa powder and melted butter into a large bowl and mix well. Press the biscuit mixture evenly over the base of the prepared tin.

Put the mascarpone and sugar into a bowl and stir in the orange juice and rind. Add the melted chocolate and brandy, and mix together until thoroughly combined. Spread the chocolate mixture evenly over the biscuit layer. Cover with clingfilm and chill for at least 4 hours.

Remove the cheesecake from the refrigerator and turn out on to a serving platter. Serve immediately.

BASE

4 tbsp butter, melted,
  plus extra for greasing
115 g/4 oz digestive biscuits,
  finely crushed
2 tsp unsweetened cocoa
  powder

CHOCOLATE LAYER

800 g/1 lb 12 oz mascarpone
  cheese
200 g/7 oz icing sugar, sifted
juice of ½ orange
finely grated rind of 1 orange
175 g/6 oz dark chocolate,
  melted
2 tbsp brandy

Brownie Bottom Cheesecake

SERVES 12

Preheat the oven to 180°C/350°F/Gas Mark 4. Lightly grease and flour a 23-cm/9-inch square baking tin.

Melt the butter and chocolate in a saucepan over a low heat, stirring often, until smooth. Remove from the heat and beat in the sugar.

Add the eggs and milk, beating well. Stir in the flour, mixing just until blended. Spoon into the prepared tin, spreading evenly.

Bake in the oven for 25 minutes. Remove from the oven while preparing the topping. Reduce the oven temperature to 160°C/325°F/Gas Mark 3.

For the topping, beat together the cheese, sugar, eggs and vanilla essence until well blended. Stir in the yogurt, then pour over the brownie base. Bake for a further 45–55 minutes or until the centre is almost set.

Run a knife around the edge of the cake to loosen from the tin. Leave to cool before removing from the tin. Chill in the refrigerator for 4 hours or overnight before cutting into slices. Serve drizzled with melted chocolate.

115 g/4 oz unsalted butter,
  plus extra for greasing
115 g/4 oz plain chocolate
200 g/7 oz caster sugar
2 eggs, beaten
50 ml /2 fl oz milk
115 g/4 oz plain flour, plus extra
  for dusting

TOPPING
500 g/1 lb 2 oz soft cheese
125 g/4½ oz caster sugar
3 eggs, beaten
1 tsp vanilla essence
125 ml/4 fl oz natural yogurt
plain chocolate, melted,
  to drizzle

Chocolate Trifle

SERVES 8

Cut the cake into slices and make 'sandwiches' with the raspberry jam. Cut the 'sandwiches' into cubes and place in a large glass serving bowl. Sprinkle with amaretto. Spread the fruit over the cake.

To make the custard, put the egg yolks and sugar in a bowl and whisk until thick and pale. Stir in the cornflour. Put the milk in a saucepan and heat until almost boiling. Pour on to the yolk mixture, stirring. Return the mixture to . the saucepan and bring just to the boil, stirring constantly until it thickens. Remove from the heat and leave to cool slightly. Put the chocolate in a bowl set over a saucepan of simmering water until melted, then add to the custard. Pour over the cake and fruit. Cool, cover and chill for 2 hours to set.

Put the cream in a bowl and whip until soft peaks form. Beat in the sugar and vanilla. Spoon over the trifle. Decorate with truffles and chocolate shapes and then chill until ready to serve.

280 g/10 oz ready-made
  chocolate loaf cake
3–4 tbsp seedless raspberry jam
4 tbsp amaretto
250 g/9 oz packet frozen
  mixed red fruit, thawed

CHOCOLATE CUSTARD
6 egg yolks
55 g/2 oz caster sugar
1 tbsp cornflour
500 ml/18 fl oz milk
55 g/2 oz dark chocolate,
  broken into pieces

TOPPING
225 ml/8 fl oz double cream
1 tbsp caster sugar
1/2 tsp vanilla essence

TO DECORATE
ready-made chocolate truffles
chocolate shapes

Chocolate Rum Pots

MAKES 6

Put the chocolate in a heatproof bowl set over a saucepan of gently simmering water until melted. Leave to cool slightly.

Whisk the egg yolks with the caster sugar in a clean bowl until very pale and fluffy.

Drizzle the melted chocolate into the mixture and fold in together with the rum and the double cream.

Whisk the egg whites in a greasefree bowl until soft peaks form. Fold the egg whites into the chocolate mixture in 2 batches. Divide the mixture among 6 individual dishes and chill in the refrigerator for at least 2 hours.

To serve, decorate with a little whipped cream and marbled chocolate shapes.

225 g/8 oz plain chocolate
4 eggs, separated
6 tbsp caster sugar
4 tbsp dark rum
4 tbsp double cream

TO DECORATE
whipped cream
marbled chocolate shapes

Chocolate Mint Swirls

SERVES 6

Place the cream in a large mixing bowl and whisk until soft peaks form.

Fold in the mascarpone cheese and icing sugar, then place about one-third of the mixture in a smaller bowl. Stir the crème de menthe into the smaller bowl. Put the plain chocolate in a heatproof bowl set over a saucepan of gently simmering water until melted. Stir the melted chocolate into the remaining mascarpone mixture.

Place alternate tablespoonfuls of the 2 mixtures into serving glasses, then swirl the mixture together to give a decorative effect. Chill until required.

To make the piped chocolate pieces decorations, melt a small amount of chocolate and place in a paper piping bag.

Place a sheet of greaseproof paper on a cutting board and pipe squiggles, stars or flower shapes on to it with the melted chocolate. Alternatively, to make curved decorations, pipe decorations on to a long strip of baking paper, then carefully place the strip over a rolling pin, securing with sticky tape. Let the chocolate set, then carefully remove from the baking paper.

Decorate each dessert with the piped chocolate decorations and serve. The desserts can be decorated and then chilled, if preferred.

300 ml/10 fl oz double cream
150 g/5½ oz mascarpone cheese
2 tbsp icing sugar
1 tbsp crème de menthe
175 g/6 oz plain chocolate, broken into pieces, plus extra to decorate

Chocolate & Vanilla Creams

MAKES 4

Place the cream and sugar in a saucepan and add the vanilla pod. Heat gently, stirring until the sugar has dissolved, then bring to the boil. Reduce the heat and simmer for 2–3 minutes.

Remove the saucepan from the heat and take out the vanilla pod. Stir in the crème fraîche.

Sprinkle the gelatine over the water in a small heatproof bowl and let it go spongy, then set over a saucepan of hot water and stir until dissolved. Stir into the cream mixture. Pour half of this mixture into another mixing bowl.

Put the plain chocolate in a heatproof bowl over a saucepan of simmering water until melted. Stir the melted chocolate into one half of the cream mixture. Pour the chocolate mixture into 4 individual glasses or glass serving dishes and chill for 15–20 minutes, until just set. While the chocolate mixture is chilling, keep the vanilla mixture at room temperature.

Spoon the vanilla mixture on top of the chocolate mixture and chill until the vanilla cream is set. When ready to serve, decorate with the chopped caraque.

450 ml/16 fl oz double cream
6 tbsp caster sugar
1 vanilla pod
200 ml/7 fl oz crème fraîche
2 tsp powdered gelatine
3 tbsp water
50 g/1¾ oz plain chocolate, broken into pieces
marbled chocolate caraque, chopped, to decorate

Raspberry Chocolate Boxes

MAKES 12

To make the mocha mousse, melt 55 g/2 oz of the chocolate in a heatproof bowl set over a saucepan of gently simmering water. Add the coffee and stir over a low heat until smooth, then remove from the heat and cool slightly. Stir in the egg yolk and the coffee liqueur. Whisk the egg whites in a separate bowl until stiff peaks form. Fold into the chocolate mixture, cover with clingfilm and chill for 2 hours, until set.

For the sponge cake, lightly grease a 20-cm/8-inch square cake tin and line the base with greaseproof paper. Put the egg and extra white with the sugar in a heatproof bowl set over a saucepan of gently simmering water. Whisk over a low heat for 5–10 minutes, until pale and thick. Remove from the heat and continue whisking for 10 minutes until cold and a trail is left when the whisk is dragged across the surface.

Preheat the oven to 180°C/350°F/Gas Mark 4. Sift the flour over the egg mixture and gently fold it in. Pour the mixture into the prepared tin and spread evenly. Bake in the preheated oven for 20–25 minutes, until firm to the touch. Turn out on to a wire rack to cool, then invert the cake, leaving the greaseproof paper in place.

To make the chocolate boxes, grease a 30 x 23-cm/12 x 9-inch Swiss roll tin and line with greaseproof paper. Place the remaining chocolate in a heatproof bowl set over a saucepan of simmering water. Stir over a low heat until melted, but not too runny. Pour into the pan and spread evenly with a spatula. Leave in a cool place for about 30 minutes, until set.

Turn out the set chocolate on to greaseproof paper on a work surface. Cut it into 36 rectangles, measuring about 7.5 x 2.5 cm/3 x 1 inches. Cut 12 of these rectangles in half to make 24 rectangles measuring about 4 x 2.5 cm/1$\frac{1}{2}$ x 1 inches.

Trim the edges off the sponge cake, then cut it into 12 slices, measuring 7.5 x 3 cm/3 x 1$\frac{1}{4}$-inches. Spread a little of the mocha mousse along the sides of each sponge rectangle and press 2 long and 2 short chocolate rectangles on to the sides to make boxes. Divide the remaining mousse among the boxes and top with raspberries. Chill until ready to serve.

MOCHA MOUSSE

200 g/7 oz plain chocolate,
   broken into pieces
1$\frac{1}{2}$ tsp cold, strong black coffee
1 egg yolk
1$\frac{1}{2}$ tsp Kahlùa or other coffee
   liqueur
2 egg whites
200 g/7 oz raspberries

SPONGE CAKE

2 tsp butter, for greasing
1 egg, plus 1 egg white
4 tbsp caster sugar
5 tbsp plain flour

Cool Minty Chocolate

MAKES 6

Pour half the milk into a small saucepan and stir in the drinking chocolate powder. Heat gently, stirring constantly, until just below boiling point and the mixture is smooth. Remove the saucepan from the heat.

Pour the chocolate-flavoured milk into a large, chilled bowl and whisk in the remaining milk. Whisk in the cream and peppermint essence and continue to whisk until cold.

Pour the mixture into 6 glasses, top each with a scoop of ice cream, decorate with a mint sprig and serve immediately.

600 ml/1 pint ice-cold milk
6 tbsp drinking chocolate
  powder
200 g/7 oz single cream
1 tsp peppermint essence
6 scoops of chocolate-mint
  ice cream
fresh mint sprigs, to decorate

Chocolate Milk Shakes

SERVES 4

Pour the milk, chocolate syrup and coffee syrup into a food processor or blender and gently process until blended. Add the ice cream and process to a smooth consistency.

Pour into glasses.

To decorate, spoon the cream into a piping bag with a large, star-shaped nozzle. Pipe generous amounts of cream on top of the milk shakes. Dust with the cocoa powder and serve.

300 ml/10 fl oz milk
2 tbsp chocolate syrup
2 tbsp coffee syrup
800 g/1 lb 12 oz chocolate ice cream

TO DECORATE
150 ml/5 fl oz double cream, whipped
cocoa powder, for dusting

Little Treats & Luxury Drinks

Chocolate Almond Petits Fours

MAKES 16

Preheat the oven to 190°C/375°F/Gas Mark 5. Line a baking tray with greaseproof paper. Put the ground almonds, sugar and cocoa powder in a bowl and mix together well. Add the egg white and mix to form a firm mixture.

Fill a piping bag, fitted with a small plain nozzle, with the mixture and pipe 5-cm/2-inch lengths, spaced well apart, on to the prepared baking tray. Place an almond half on top of each.

Bake in the oven for about 5 minutes, until firm. Transfer to a wire rack and leave to cool.

When the petits fours are cold, melt the chocolate in a heatproof bowl set over a saucepan of gently simmering water. Dip each end of the petits fours into the melted chocolate, then leave on the wire rack to set.

40 g/1½ oz ground almonds

85 g/3 oz granulated sugar

5 tsp cocoa powder

1 egg white

8 blanched almonds, halved

55 g/2 oz plain chocolate, broken into pieces

Ginger Chocolate Fudge

MAKES AROUND 50 PIECES

Grease an 18-cm/7-inch square, shallow tin or a 20 x 15-cm/8 x 6-inch rectangular, shallow tin. Dry the syrup off the pieces of stem ginger on kitchen paper, then chop finely.

Pour the milk into a large, heavy-based saucepan and add the chocolate, butter and sugar. Heat gently, stirring all the time, until the chocolate and butter have melted and the sugar has completely dissolved.

Bring to the boil and boil for about 10–15 minutes, stirring occasionally, until a little of the mixture, when dropped into a small bowl of cold water, forms a soft ball when rolled between the fingers.

Remove the saucepan from the heat and stir in the chopped ginger. Leave to cool for 5 minutes, then beat the mixture vigorously with a wooden spoon, until thick, creamy and grainy.

Immediately pour the mixture into the prepared tin, leave to cool, then mark into small squares. Leave the fudge until cold and set, then cut up the squares with a sharp knife.

115 g/4 oz butter, plus extra for greasing
6 pieces stem ginger
300 ml/10 fl oz milk
150 g/5½ oz plain chocolate, broken into pieces
450 g/1 lb granulated sugar

Fruit & Nut Fudge

MAKES 36 PIECES

Lightly grease a 20-cm/8-inch square cake tin.

Put the chocolate in a heatproof bowl with the butter and evaporated milk and set over a saucepan of gently simmering water. Stir until the chocolate and butter have melted and the mixture is well blended.

Remove the bowl from the heat and gradually beat in the icing sugar. Stir the hazelnuts and sultanas into the mixture. Press the fudge into the prepared tin and smooth the top. Chill until firm.

Tip the fudge out on to a chopping board and cut into squares. Chill in the refrigerator until required.

2 tbsp butter, plus extra for greasing
250 g/9 oz plain chocolate, broken into pieces
4 tbsp evaporated milk
460 g/1 lb icing sugar, sifted
50 g/1¾ oz roughly chopped hazelnuts
50 g/1¾ oz sultanas

Chocolate Creams

MAKES ABOUT 30

Line a baking tray with greaseproof paper. Melt 55 g/2 oz of the chocolate in a large heatproof bowl set over a saucepan of gently simmering water. Stir in the cream and remove the bowl from the heat.

Sift the icing sugar into the melted chocolate then, using a fork, mix together well. Knead to form a firm, smooth, pliable mixture.

Lightly dust a work surface with drinking chocolate powder, turn out the mixture, and roll out to a 5-mm/^{1}/$_4$-inch thickness, then cut into rounds, using a 2.5-cm/1-inch plain round cutter.

Transfer to the prepared baking tray and leave to stand for about 12 hours, or overnight, until set and dry.

When the chocolate creams have set, line a baking tray with greaseproof paper. Melt the remaining chocolate in a heatproof bowl set over a saucepan of gently simmering water. Using 2 forks, carefully dip each chocolate cream into the melted chocolate. Lift it out quickly, letting any excess chocolate drain against the side of the bowl, and place on the prepared baking tray. Leave to set.

200 g/7 oz plain chocolate, broken into pieces
2 tbsp single cream
225 g/8 oz icing sugar
cocoa powder, for dusting

Nutty Chocolate Clusters

MAKES 30

Line a baking tray with a sheet of greaseproof paper. Put the white chocolate in a large heatproof bowl set over a saucepan of gently simmering water and stir until melted.

Break the digestive biscuits into small pieces. Stir the crumbs into the melted chocolate with the chopped nuts, and stem ginger if using.

Place heaped teaspoons of the mixture on the prepared baking tray.

Chill the mixture until set, then remove from the greaseproof paper.

Melt the plain chocolate as above and let it cool slightly. Dip the clusters into the melted chocolate, allowing the excess to drip back into the bowl. Return the clusters to the baking tray and chill in the refrigerator until set.

175 g/6 oz white chocolate, broken into pieces
100 g/3½ oz digestive biscuits
100 g/3½ oz chopped macadamia nuts or Brazil nuts
25 g/1 oz stem ginger, chopped (optional)
175 g/6 oz plain chocolate, broken into pieces

Mini Florentines

MAKES 40

Preheat the oven to 180°C/350°F/Gas Mark 4. Grease and flour 2 baking trays or line with greaseproof paper.

Place the butter in a small saucepan and heat gently until melted. Add the sugar, stir until dissolved, then bring the mixture to the boil. Remove from the heat and stir in the sultanas, cherries, ginger, sunflower seeds and almonds. Mix well, then beat in the cream.

Place small teaspoons of the fruit and nut mixture on to the prepared baking trays, allowing plenty of room for the mixture to spread during baking. Bake in the preheated oven for 10–12 minutes, or until light golden in colour.

Remove from the oven and, while still hot, use a circular biscuit cutter to pull in the edges to form perfect circles. Leave to cool and go crisp before removing from the baking trays.

Put the chocolate in a heatproof bowl set over a saucepan of gently simmering water and stir until melted. Spread most of the chocolate on to a sheet of greaseproof paper. When the chocolate is on the point of setting, place the biscuits flat-side down on the chocolate and let it harden completely.

Cut around the florentines and remove from the greaseproof paper. Spread a little more chocolate on the coated side of the florentines and use a fork to mark waves in the chocolate. Leave to set. Keep cool.

6 tbsp butter, plus extra for
   greasing
plain flour, for dusting
75 g/2¾ oz caster sugar
2 tbsp sultanas or raisins
2 tbsp chopped glacé cherries
2 tbsp chopped stem ginger
25 g/1 oz sunflower seeds
100 g/3½ oz flaked almonds
2 tbsp double cream
175 g/6 oz plain or milk
   chocolate, broken into pieces

Hot Chocolate Cherries

SERVES 4

Put the water, sugar and lemon rind into a heavy-based saucepan and bring to the boil over a low heat, stirring constantly until the sugar has dissolved. Add the cherries and cook, stirring constantly, for 1 minute. Remove the saucepan from the heat and, using a slotted spoon, transfer the cherries to a flameproof dish. Reserve the syrup.

Preheat the grill to medium. Put the cocoa powder in a bowl and mix in a pinch of salt. Whisking constantly, pour in the cream in a steady stream. Remove and discard the lemon rind from the syrup, then stir in the cream mixture. Return the pan to the heat and bring to the boil, stirring constantly. Simmer over a very low heat, stirring occasionally, for 10–15 minutes, or until reduced by about half.

Remove from the heat, stir in the maraschino liqueur and pour the sauce over the cherries. Place under the preheated grill for 2 minutes, then serve.

4 tbsp water
55 g/2 oz caster sugar
1 strip pared lemon rind
450 g/1 lb sweet black cherries, stoned
1 tbsp cocoa powder
salt
4 tbsp double cream
4 tbsp maraschino liqueur or cherry brandy

White Chocolate Truffles

MAKES 20

Line a Swiss roll tin with greaseproof paper.

Place the butter and cream in a small saucepan and bring slowly to the boil, stirring constantly. Boil for 1 minute, then remove from the heat.

Add the chocolate to the cream. Stir until melted, then beat in the liqueur if using.

Pour into the prepared tin and chill for about 2 hours until firm.

Break off pieces of the mixture and roll them into balls. Chill for an additional 30 minutes before finishing the truffles.

To finish, put the white chocolate in a heatproof bowl set over a saucepan of gently simmering water until melted. Dip the balls in the chocolate, letting the excess drip back into the bowl. Place on non-stick baking paper, swirl the chocolate with the tines of a fork, and let it harden.

2 tbsp unsalted butter

5 tbsp double cream

225 g/8 oz good-quality Swiss white chocolate, broken into pieces

1 tbsp orange liqueur (optional)

100 g/3½ oz white chocolate, broken into pieces, for coating

Italian Chocolate Truffles

MAKES 24

Melt the plain chocolate with the amaretto or orange liqueur in a heatproof bowl set over a saucepan of gently simmering water, stirring until well combined.

Add the butter and stir until it has melted. Stir in the icing sugar and the ground almonds.

Leave the mixture in a cool place until firm enough to roll into 24 balls.

Place the grated chocolate on a plate and roll the truffles in the chocolate to coat them.

Place the truffles in paper sweet cases and chill.

175 g/6 oz plain chocolate, broken into pieces
2 tbsp amaretto or orange liqueur
3 tbsp unsalted butter
4 tbsp icing sugar
50 g/1¾ oz ground almonds
50 g/1¾ oz grated chocolate

Chocolate Liqueurs

MAKES 40

Line a baking tray with a sheet of greaseproof paper. Put the plain chocolate in a heatproof bowl and set over a saucepan of gently simmering water. Stir until melted. Spoon the chocolate into 40 paper sweet cases, spreading up the sides with a spoon or brush. Place upside down on the baking tray and leave to set.

Carefully peel away the paper cases. Place a cherry or nut in each cup.

To make the filling, place the double cream in a mixing bowl and sift the icing sugar on top. Whisk the cream until it is just holding its shape, then whisk in the liqueur.

Place the cream in a piping bag fitted with a 1-cm/½-inch plain nozzle and pipe a little into each chocolate case. Leave to chill for 20 minutes.

To decorate, spoon the plain chocolate over the cream to cover it. Add the caraque and let it harden.

100 g/3½ oz plain chocolate,
 broken into pieces
20 glacé cherries
20 hazelnuts or macadamia nuts
150 ml/5 fl oz double cream
2 tbsp icing sugar
4 tbsp liqueur

TO DECORATE
50 g/1¾ oz plain chocolate,
 melted
marbled chocolate caraque

Rum & Chocolate Cups

MAKES 12

To make the chocolate cups, place the chocolate in a heatproof bowl set over a saucepan of gently simmering water. Stir over a low heat until the chocolate is just melted but not too runny, then remove from the heat. Spoon about $^1/_2$ teaspoon of melted chocolate into a foil sweet case and brush it over the base and up the sides. Coat 11 more foil cases in the same way and leave to set for 30 minutes. Chill in the refrigerator for 15 minutes. If necessary, reheat the chocolate in the heatproof bowl to melt it again, then coat the foil cases with a second, slightly thinner coating. Let the cases chill in the refrigerator for an additional 30 minutes.

Meanwhile, make the filling. Place the chocolate in a heatproof bowl set over a saucepan of gently simmering water. Stir over a low heat until melted, then remove from the heat. Leave to cool slightly, then stir in the rum and beat in the mascarpone cheese until fully incorporated and smooth. Leave to cool completely, stirring occasionally.

Spoon the filling into a piping bag fitted with a 1-cm/$^1/_2$-inch star nozzle. If preferred, carefully peel away the foil cases from the chocolate cups. Pipe the filling into the cups and top each one with a toasted hazelnut.

55 g/2 oz plain chocolate, broken into pieces
12 toasted hazelnuts

FILLING
115 g/4 oz plain chocolate, broken into pieces
1 tbsp dark rum
4 tbsp mascarpone cheese

Rocky Road Bites

MAKES 18

Line a baking tray with greaseproof paper and set aside.

Put the milk chocolate in a large heatproof bowl. Set the bowl over a saucepan of gently simmering water and stir until the chocolate has melted.

Stir in the marshmallows, walnuts and apricots, and toss in the melted chocolate until well covered.

Put heaped teaspoonfuls of the mixture on the prepared baking tray.

Let the sweets chill in the refrigerator until set.

Once set, carefully remove the sweets from the greaseproof paper.

Place in paper sweet cases to serve, if desired.

125 g/4$\frac{1}{2}$ oz milk chocolate, broken into pieces
40 g/1$\frac{1}{2}$ oz mini multi-coloured marshmallows
25 g/1 oz chopped walnuts
25 g/1 oz ready-to-eat dried apricots, chopped

Apricot & Almond Clusters

MAKES 24–28

Put the chocolate and honey in a heatproof bowl set over a saucepan of gently simmering water and stir until melted and smooth.

Stir in the apricots and almonds.

Drop teaspoonfuls of the mixture into paper sweet cases. Leave to set.

115 g/4 oz plain chocolate, broken into pieces
2 tbsp clear honey
115 g/4 oz ready-to-eat dried apricots, chopped
55 g/2 oz blanched almonds, chopped

Brazil Nut Brittle

MAKES 20

Brush the bottom of a 20-cm/8-inch square cake tin with oil and line with greaseproof paper. Put half the plain chocolate in a heatproof bowl and set over a saucepan of gently simmering water. Stir until melted, then spread in the prepared tin.

Sprinkle with the chopped Brazil nuts, white chocolate and fudge. Melt the remaining plain chocolate pieces and pour over the top.

Let the brittle set, then break up into jagged pieces using the tip of a strong knife.

sunflower oil, for brushing

350 g/12 oz plain chocolate, broken into pieces

100 g/3½ oz shelled Brazil nuts, chopped

175 g/6 oz white chocolate, roughly chopped

175 g/6 oz fudge, roughly chopped

Chocolate Fondue

SERVES 6

Using a sharp knife, peel and core the pineapple, then cut the flesh into cubes. Peel the mango and cut the flesh into cubes. Peel back the papery outer skin of the physalis and twist at the top to make a 'handle'. Arrange all the fruit on 6 serving plates and leave to chill in the refrigerator.

To make the fondue, place the chocolate and cream in a fondue pot. Heat gently, stirring constantly, until the chocolate has melted. Stir in the brandy until thoroughly blended and the chocolate mixture is smooth.

Place the fondue pot over the burner to keep warm. To serve, allow each guest to dip the fruit into the sauce, using fondue forks or bamboo skewers.

1 pineapple
1 mango
12 physalis
250 g/9 oz fresh strawberries
250 g/9 oz seedless green
   grapes

FONDUE
250 g/9 oz plain chocolate,
   broken into pieces
150 ml/5 fl oz double cream
2 tbsp brandy

French Chocolate Sauce

SERVES 2–4

Bring the cream gently to the boil in a small, heavy-based saucepan over a low heat. Remove the saucepan from the heat, add the broken chocolate and stir until smooth.

Stir in the liqueur and serve immediately, or keep the sauce warm until required. Serve over ice cream.

6 tbsp double cream
85 g/3 oz dark chocolate, broken into small pieces
2 tbsp orange liqueur
ice cream, to serve

Chocolate Fudge Sauce

SERVES 2–4

Pour the cream into the top of a double boiler or a heatproof bowl set over a saucepan of gently simmering water. Add the butter and sugar and stir until the mixture is smooth. Remove from the heat.

Stir in the chocolate, a few pieces at a time, waiting until each batch has melted before adding the next. Add the brandy and stir the sauce until smooth. Cool to room temperature before serving.

150 ml/5 fl oz double cream

4 tbsp butter, cut into small pieces

3 tbsp caster sugar

175 g/6 oz white chocolate, broken into pieces

2 tbsp brandy

Real Hot Chocolate

SERVES 1–2

Place the chocolate in a large, heatproof jug. Place the milk in a heavy-based saucepan and bring to the boil. Pour about one-quarter of the milk on to the chocolate and leave until the chocolate has softened.

Whisk the milk and chocolate mixture until smooth. Return the remaining milk to the heat and return to the boil, then pour on to the chocolate, whisking constantly.

Pour into warmed mugs or cups and decorate with chocolate curls. Serve immediately.

40 g/1½ oz plain chocolate, broken into pieces
300 ml/10 fl oz milk
chocolate curls, to decorate

Hot Chocolate Float

SERVES 4

Pour the milk into a saucepan. Break the chocolate into small pieces and add to the saucepan with the sugar. Stir over a low heat until the chocolate has melted, the sugar has dissolved and the mixture is smooth. Remove the saucepan from the heat.

Put 1 scoop of coconut ice cream into each of 4 heatproof glasses, top with a scoop of chocolate ice cream, then repeat the layers.

Pour the chocolate-flavoured milk into the glasses, top with whipped cream and serve immediately.

450 ml/16 fl oz milk
225 g/8 oz plain chocolate
2 tbsp caster sugar
8 scoops coconut ice cream
8 scoops plain chocolate ice cream
whipped cream, to decorate

Cinnamon Mocha

SERVES 6

Put the chocolate in a large heatproof bowl set over a saucepan of gently simmering water. Add the cream and stir until the chocolate has melted and the mixture is smooth.

Pour in the coffee, add the cinnamon, and whisk until foamy. If serving hot, pour into heatproof glasses or mugs, top with cream and caraque, and serve immediately. If serving cold, remove the bowl from the heat and leave to cool, chill in the refrigerator until required, then decorate with whipped cream, a sprinkling of ground cinnamon, and the caraque.

250 g/9 oz milk chocolate, broken into pieces
175 ml/6 fl oz single cream
1 litre/1¾ pints freshly brewed coffee
1 tsp ground cinnamon, plus extra to decorate

TO DECORATE
whipped cream
marbled chocolate caraque

Marshmallow Float

SERVES 4

Finely chop the chocolate with a knife or in a food processor. Do not over-process or the chocolate will melt.

Pour the milk into a saucepan and bring to just below boiling point. Remove the saucepan from the heat and whisk in the sugar and the chocolate.

Pour into warmed mugs or heatproof glasses, top with marshmallows and serve immediately.

225 g/8 oz plain chocolate, broken into pieces
900 ml/1½ pints milk
3 tbsp caster sugar
8 marshmallows